Religious Diversity

Religious Diversity

Wilfred Cantwell Smith

Edited by Willard G. Oxtoby

CROSSROAD · NEW YORK

1982
The Crossroad Publishing Company
575 Lexington Avenue, New York, N.Y. 10022

Published by arrangement with Harper & Row, Publishers, Inc.

Printed in the United States of America

Library of Congress Catalog Card Number: 81-70382

ISBN 0-8245-0458-5

Contents

Editor's Introduction   vii

PART ONE
Religious Diversity and Truth

1. The Christian in a Religiously Plural World   3
2. Is the Qur'an the Word of God?   22
3. The Study of Religion and the Study of the Bible   41

PART TWO
Religious Diversity and Modernity

4. Traditional Religions and Modern Culture   59
5. The Meaning of Modernization   77
6. Mankind's Religiously Divided History Approaches
   Self-Consciousness   96

PART THREE
Religious Diversity and Mutual Understanding

7. Participation: The Changing Christian Role in Other
   Cultures   117
8. Comparative Religion: Whither—and Why?   138
9. Objectivity and the Humane Sciences: A New Proposal   158

For Further Reading   181

Index   195

Editor's Introduction

"Before I met Wilfred, I had studied Buddhism as a system. What I learned from him was to look for the faith of Buddhists as persons." These words, from one of Wilfred Cantwell Smith's Harvard students, sum up as succinctly as any the influence of this Canadian scholar, by general consent one of the foremost in the "history of religions," or comparative religion, field.

In the past twenty-five years, in three successive appointments at McGill (Montreal), Harvard, and Dalhousie (Halifax) universities, as well as through his publications, Smith has exerted a subtle but considerable influence on the academic study of religion in general and of Islam in particular. Some of the points he has stressed have been historical observations about the subject-matter, tracing the development of particular institutions or ideas. But what for many stands out as distinctive is his concern for the student's role in addressing the subject-matter—the responsibilities one takes on when dealing with the living, vital faith of other human beings. To approach the faith of others is to enter into a human encounter, where "understanding" is not a cold abstraction but a matter of mutual dialogue.

The purpose of this collection is to introduce the beginner to Smith's thought through a sampling of nine of his shorter writings. The essays selected present his views, over a sixteen-year period, relating to the general study of religion; his specialized work in Islamic studies is outside the domain of this collection. I present Smith's views in the spirit of a friend: "friend" rather than "colleague," since, though we taught in the same faculty in the early 1960's, I would think it presumptuous to claim any share in his accomplishments; and "friend" rather than "pupil," since, though I have learned much from Smith, I could not acknowledge a degree of dependence on the total structure of his thought to the extent that discipleship would require.

As editor I have in a sense tried to think Smith's thoughts with him and to present his spirit and intent. To make this an introductory volume, however, I have proposed more changes than editors sometimes do. There are, in fact, several hundred deviations from the previously published texts of these essays, most of them of a stylistic nature and quite minor, but some of them not. Some essays have been condensed by as much as one-third, and footnotes have been eliminated except for the sources of direct quotations. The changes have received what Smith calls his "acquiescence," no small matter in the case of a scholar who rightly insists on strict accuracy of citation and quotation in his students' work as well as his own. Such a scholar has every right to be scandalized at having his work "filtered" through another writer's sense of argument or usage. For the defects which may have resulted from abridgment and alteration, then, the editor alone stands accountable.

BIOGRAPHICAL REMARKS

Wilfred Smith is a Torontonian who lived in his native city until graduation at twenty-one from the University except for overseas travel, and who in his adult life has lived elsewhere except to return for one sabbatical year. More importantly, he is a Canadian who during his years of residence in Britain, in the Indian subcontinent, and in the United States always has maintained touch with the academic and religious life of his native land.

Smith was born in Toronto on July 21, 1916, the younger of two sons of the managing director of the Swan Pen Company of Canada, and later the Parker Pen Company of Canada. Between the ages of eight and seventeen he attended Upper Canada College, the English-style boys' preparatory school whose tower at the head of Avenue Road stands as a midtown landmark. Upper Canada College has claimed among its alumni many leaders in the life of the province and of the country, and the Smith brothers were no exception. Alongside Wilfred's distinguished scholarly career may be mentioned the career of Arnold Cantwell Smith in the Canadian diplomatic service, including ambassadorships in Cairo and Moscow, and the Secretary-Generalship of the British Commonwealth.

The Toronto of Smith's boyhood was distinctly different from the bustling, ethnically diverse metropolis which the city has become especially since the mid-1960's. In the years before the Second World War it was a relatively small city, very British, and very observantly religious. Stories abound concerning Toronto in those prewar years, when Sunday-closing legislation was strictly enforced and a Sunday visitor to downtown would have the streets to himself, lucky even to be able to buy a cup of tea. "Toronto the Good," the city was nicknamed, and it earned its sobriquet in part through earnestness and seriousness of purpose, honesty and quality in workmanship, and a quiet courtesy and dignity in conduct—all traits which received strong emphasis in the Smith household. In one notable respect, though, the Smith ethos was not typically Torontonian: the marked internationalism and warm welcome to persons from other cultures contrasts with the clannishness of a city where even today the three Torontonians in every eight who were born outside Canada have few close social contacts with the Canadian-born five.

The Smiths were Presbyterians; the family was active in Knox Presbyterian Church, just west of the University campus. The religious dedication of the family was one of both belief and practice. Partly because of his mother's Methodist background, Wilfred would mention "of feeling" as well, perhaps a less ob-

servable trait: one lifelong friend described Wilfred as "pious—
that is, disciplined in his religious faith but without being outwardly emotional." On the doctrinal side, certain classic formulations which Smith as a young man took fairly literally he would
later reject and then come intellectually to view as symbolic, but
symbolic always of a profound transcendent reality. Faith, the
quality of the individual's lived, ongoing relationship with God
or the transcendent, is very much a personal reality for Smith,
and very much in keeping with Reformation individualism.
While some of Smith's doctrinal views in young adulthood became quite unorthodox (for example his unwillingness to confine God's grace and salvation to Christendom), he has maintained a discipline in his personal life which would have to be
called orthoprax: a scrupulous personal morality coupled with
reverent Sunday observance and abstinence from several common
forms of self-indulgence. As he says in the seventh essay in this
anthology, "I . . . will never shake off my delightful Calvinistic
Puritanism until the day I die."

Yet, as he goes on immediately to say, his primary community
is not the Presbyterian but the Christian. The priority of
ecumenical concerns was expressed in Smith's student days chiefly
in the contexts of overseas missions and university campuses. Interdenominational collaboration in missions, where historical
divisions of European Christianity made little sense, had advanced early in the twentieth century with the formation of the
International Missionary Council, and would contribute sub-
stantially to the formation in 1948 of the World Council of
Churches. Meanwhile, in American universities, the Student
Volunteer Movement (S.V.M.) for Foreign Missions engaged the
loyalties of Protestant students across denominational lines.
Smith, a thoughtful and earnest leader, was active in the S.V.M.
at Toronto, and also in the other principal interdenominational
campus activity, the Student Christian Movement, of which he
became president in 1937. His university friends included the
children and grandchildren of missionaries to Asia. One of these
was Muriel MacKenzie Struthers, whom Smith married in 1939.

During Smith's youth the issue of church union on the Canadian domestic scene was an urgent one, as Canada's Methodists and Congregationalists were joined by roughly half of the Presbyterians in 1925 to form the United Church of Canada, while the remainder of the denomination continued apart. It was in the "continuing Presbyterian" church that Smith's father was an elder, and in his undergraduate days Smith developed United Church involvements also. In going to Britain for theological study, however, Wilfred did not have to choose one church over the other, and his ordination to an interdenominationally supported assignment in India in 1943 was one which the Presbyterian Church of Canada promptly recognized by placing him on their roll of ministers, where he would remain for seventeen years. The 1950's saw Smith involved in the joint academic venture of the Faculty of Divinity at McGill, and his family participating in a United Church congregation. After some years in which critical concerns held priority, Smith, receiving an encouraging response in 1961 to his proposals of a more open Christian attitude toward the religions of Asia, decided to take a more active role in theological leadership and transferred his ordination to the United Church of Canada.

Fully as important as the character of Smith's religious participation for an understanding of his work is his dedication to scholarship in the humanistic tradition. To his school years at Upper Canada College and a year spent at the age of eleven at the Lycée Champollion in Grenoble, France, one may ascribe a strong emphasis on precision in the use of language and accuracy in historical documentation. His undergraduate years at University College in the University of Toronto were spent in a well-focused "honours" B.A. program in "Oriental" studies, that is, the classical Semitic languages and Near Eastern history, a field which has always been strong at Toronto. With this type of specialization, Smith has always tended to employ the particulars of historical detail as a check on general philosophical theories—his own or anyone else's.

Following his graduation from Toronto, Smith studied theology in Britain for two years at Westminster College, Cambridge, while at the same time pursuing Arabic and Islamic studies with Hamilton A. R. Gibb as a research student in Oriental languages at St. John's College, Cambridge University. In 1941, as the Second World War deepened, Smith went to India and the next year became the representative among Muslims of the Canadian Overseas Missions Council, an appointment he held until going to McGill. He was based mainly in the Islamic city of Lahore, where for much of his stay he taught Indian history at Forman Christian College, and was affiliated with the University of the Panjab. Smith returned to North America after the war to complete a doctorate in the Department of Oriental Languages of Princeton University, under the Arab historian Philip K. Hitti, with a doctoral dissertation entitled "The Azhar Journal: Analysis and Critique," on the Arabic monthly from Cairo's seat of Islamic orthodoxy.

Smith had spent a year in Spain and Egypt before university at the age of seventeen. This, and his years in the Indian subcontinent in his late twenties, would have a lasting effect on his outlook. The Islamic tradition, far from being a mediaeval development in a distant land, was to him the living faith of persons one numbered among one's friends and acquaintances. Christians in India seemed insufficiently conversant with Islamic realities, tempted to live in a world isolated from the mainstream of the society. For Smith the excitement and the challenge lay in his contacts with Muslim (and Hindu and Sikh) intellectuals, some of whom have in subsequent years assumed positions of leadership in the educational, journalistic, and political worlds of Pakistan and India.

Both Smith's concern for social welfare and his training as a historian found expression in his late teens and twenties in a strong affinity for Marxist thought. *Modern Islam in India: A Social Analysis* (1943), Smith's first publication, is Marxist to the extent that it sees social class as a prime explanation of belief and behavior and is optimistic about the possibility of material human betterment. In the Cold War era five years later, by which time the realities of Soviet tactics had become well known, Smith moved toward a much more critical view of Marxism, though without abandoning the understanding of history as process, nor the moral concern, which had made Marxist thought congenial.

During the twenty-five years of his mature career Smith has held three principal academic appointments.

In the first of these, Smith served for fourteen years at McGill University in Montreal, where he went at the age of thirty-three as the W. M. Birks Professor of Comparative Religion. His was a new non-ecclesiastical position which figured in the formation of the Faculty of Divinity as part of the university after three and a half decades of interdenominational theological co-operation. Two years later, in 1951, Smith organized McGill's Institute of Islamic Studies, serving as its first director in addition to continuing in his divinity chair. The time was ripe; the Institute was launched in an era when government- and foundation-sponsored area-studies programs were being set up at many American universities.

What was distinctive about Smith's McGill program is that it focused not on a geographical area like the Middle East as such, but rather, on the question of common factors of Muslim identity which bind together several cultural areas from West Africa to Central Asia and Indonesia. We now know, sometimes from the news media and sometimes in spite of them, that not all Muslims are Arabs; but a generation ago American university programs dealing with Islam largely focused on its origins and its classical Arabic phase. Even the Ottoman Turks, who had loomed large as an influence in modern European history and whose symbol the crescent had come to be used as the principal symbol of Islam, were seen as in some sense heirs of the Arabs; and Islam east of the Arab world, where the numerical majority of Muslims live, was seen as peripheral. Smith, thanks in particular to his personal contacts in India, was able to project McGill's coverage of Islam beyond the Middle East in a significant way.

Even more important to Smith in the structuring of the Institute was the proviso that half the faculty members and half the student body of graduate-degree candidates should be Muslims. This feature, to which we will return, was intended to ensure that Western and Muslim students might, through a dialogue both academic and religious, come up with mutually acceptable descriptive formulations regarding Islam.

Smith went to his second major position in 1964, when at the age of forty-eight he took up the directorship of Harvard University's Center for the Study of World Religions, an enterprise training graduate students and related to the Divinity School, which had then been functioning for about seven years. While Smith had seen his work at McGill as a bilateral dialogue between Islam and Western scholarship, his new context was that of a multilateral forum to which participants from a plurality of traditions contributed. The Divinity School context, too, made a difference: some of the Center's dialogue was explicitly with Christian theology, not simply with Western scholarship on Asia *per se*. On the Western-thought side, Smith devoted considerable effort to extending the concern of Harvard's "secular" Faculty of Arts and Sciences for the study of religion, especially at the undergraduate level. Also, in contrast to the McGill Institute pattern of living in the city and coming together during the day for study, the Harvard setting saw Smith and most of the students living in the Center residence in a shared extracurricular life and fanning out through the University for classes in various departments; the Director's household, which included his five children, thus was constantly the scene of formal colloquia and of informal counseling and hospitality.

After nine years at Harvard, Smith, then fifty-seven, resigned to go to his third major appointment, in a move which surprised many who knew the energy and the dedication with which he had been devoting himself to questions of academic policy at Harvard. Smith returned to Canada, to take up a McCulloch professorship at Dalhousie University in Halifax, and to be the first member of its religion department. Canada was an attraction in itself; another was the promise of a lighter administrative load which would permit more time for writing, including the completion of a major book on faith and belief. Smith has spoken of his move to Dalhousie also as part of an effort to look more generally at the nature of religious faith and at the interpretation of the Orient and its religious traditions in Western study, and to reflect on the nature of the Western academic heritage itself.

Thus the biographical narrative reaches the present time, and Smith the age of sixty (1976). It would be very tidy if the substance of Smith's concerns were neatly divisible into an Islamics phase at McGill, an interfaith and theological-dialogue phase at Harvard, and a period of general theoretical reflection at Dalhousie. The reader will soon perceive, however, that all these concerns have been present from an early date in Smith's intellectual life, and that substantial contributions to each of these topics had already begun to appear during his McGill years. Smith has never been content to follow simply one line of inquiry at a time.

MAJOR THEMES IN SMITH'S THOUGHT

History. Smith is by training and inclination a historian. His fascination is engaged by the rich array of human experience, recorded over centuries on several continents. Its very diversity poses a challenge for description and comprehension; its constantly changing flux poses uncertainties and opportunities for the future. What we know of history is a limited or partial mental construct: history is not only, as W. C. Sellar and R. J. Yeatman humorously remarked, "what you can remember"; history itself is a process larger and more variegated than our comprehension of it.

To Smith the task of the historian, therefore, is to appreciate the past as it has been, to seek to discern the directions in which the historical process has moved, and to build a foundation by which man may knowledgeably chart its future course. The historian must seek his understanding often by immersing himself in a rigorous and disciplined examination of source material, often scrutinizing texts in difficult languages; there are no short-cuts for proper preparation. In the study of religion this will mean that the student must not merely generalize, but should know the minute facts of a specific tradition well.

The historian is not simply a spectator. He can make his society aware of the possibilities of choice. It is this self-consciousness about the ability to shape one's destiny which, Smith has held, makes a culture modern.

Change is real. Institutions change; ideas change. The historian discovers that a pattern or a concept one might have thought fixed turns out to have been at some point an innovation—for example, that the term "religion" did not come into general use in the plural before the seventeenth century, or the name "Hinduism" before the nineteenth. And there is no reason that even a recent formulation need be perpetuated: Smith relishes novelty, seeking to put questions in new ways, or better yet to put new questions, especially if the old answers to old questions are felt to have led to an impasse.

The Intellectual's Role. The key to change, particularly to informed, conscious change, lies with the intellectuals of the world's various societies. Intellectuals are a proper subject of study, for they affect the course of history out of all proportion to their numbers. But more importantly, "intellectual" should be a description of the student himself. Smith describes his own activity as intellectual, and writes for an intellectual audience.

Certain observations may be made about proper intellectual discourse. To begin with, it is rational. To be an intellectual implies espousing a position on demonstrable and defensible grounds, and being able to offer reasons and supporting evidence for a view. Secondly, intellectual discourse should be broadly intelligible; Smith decries the fragmentation of academic discourse into the jargon and methodological abstraction of the "disciplines," preferring the ideal of communicating intelligibly with the literate, generally educated man.

Thirdly, the intellectual, be he humanist or scientist, is a man with a commitment. Traditionally, the dedication in Western culture to learning and to "truth" has been traced back to ancient Greece. The Hellenic tradition, it is often held, has given us science and philosophy—two endeavors whose names (one Latin, one Greek) etymologically connote knowledge and wisdom respectively. Though others may have found it fashionable to contrast in our heritage Athens as the source of criticism and Jerusalem as the source of commitment, Smith takes the rationalist, academic heritage as analogous to a religious tradition, which demands a form of participation and affirmation from those who bear it. The traditionally religious intellectual in the Christian West, therefore, is a man who participates simultaneously in two traditions, the rationalist and the religious. It appears to be Smith's view that such a double commitment is not only possible but requisite, and that indeed to pursue rational truth is to participate in one phase of the pursuit of divine truth.

Intercultural Contact. In our times the world has become one world, one interlocking, interacting culture, to a degree that it never was before. Intercontinental communications involve an exponentially greater number of people than even a generation ago. Travelers can now wonder whether they've left home, when in a surrealistic daze they contemplate airports and expressways and high rise apartments which look practically the same in Tokyo as in Toronto, in Cairo as in Caracas, in Lagos as in London. The transistor radio has brought most of the people of the globe into instantaneous contact with political events everywhere. And international travel, some have remarked, has had homogenizing effects which destroy one of the principal reasons for traveling.

Worldwide contact is real, and it has important consequences. What is said about Muslims or Buddhists in the West today may be read by Muslims or Buddhists in Asia tomorrow. An invidious caricature or stereotype of another culture can no longer be made with impunity as in the smug isolation which once prevailed; now the people one talks about are one's partners in

intercultural dialogue and can complain when they feel mis-
represented.

It is a mistake for the West to suppose it has all the answers.
We can distort other cultures, for example, by the subject headings or categories with which we in the West describe Asia or
classify its data. We suppose, for example, that religious tradition
is a particular factor in culture, that it denotes a particular part
of society's functioning, as over against an area which we call the
secular. But, Smith observes, how does such a dichotomy serve us
in discussing classical China (where we strain to find the explicitly religious) or the classical Islamic world (where we are hard
put to it to find the explicitly secular)? In so many ways—such
as the way we organize "non-Western" area studies, or the way
we classify books in libraries—we are simply imposing our cultural categories where they do not fit. The task of the student of
religion is in part to discern how the parts of a culture fit together into a total picture differently in a religion other than
our own.

One's own tradition can have no exclusive claim on truth.
Blatant arrogance is offensive enough in secular contexts, but it
is particularly reprehensible when voiced in the name of religion.
Traditional Christian theology, which has assumed Christendom
to have a monopoly on divine grace and salvation, is, in Smith's
judgment, morally wrong and must give way to formulations
that permit thinking of God as active through other men's traditions as well. The first essay in this collection states this challenge
tellingly. A religious pluralism is the only morally acceptable
answer in a religiously plural world. Plurality, the existence of
diversity, is a fact; pluralism, the acceptance of diversity, is an
imperative.

The Nature of Religion. Religion, for Smith, has two chief
components: cumulative tradition, and personal faith. Tradition
is easy to identify: it is externally observable, and varied in its
particulars; the phrase "cumulative tradition" is felicitous, since
it guards against any tendency to think of tradition as fixed or
static. More problematical, and closer to the heart of things, is

"faith"—in Smith's view, the outlook on life and the quality of conduct in life which the religious person maintains. Faith is never a completed, static entity that someone can "have," neatly packaged, any more than is virtue in the thought of Aristotle. Faith is a quality of being religious, each day. The religious person is a man of faith; if he is unlettered, the faith may be simple, while for the intellectual, faith obviously demands all the sophistication of which he is capable.

For Smith "faith" does not have a plural. Just as he opposes the use of "religions" in the plural because the usage implies separate entities rather than a quality of living, so he avoids speaking of "faiths," a usage which would reintroduce the same reification and segmentation he had been striving to combat in proposing to expunge "religions" from our vocabulary. In the seventh essay in this collection, where "faiths" had appeared in the original publication, Smith corrected the text to read "forms of faith."

If faith is not properly referred to as plural, any more than "religiousness" could be and for some of the same reasons, is faith then a unitary entity? This is a key question, which Smith believes he has already answered in the negative—not only by cautioning us lest we assume one person's faith to be the same as another's, but even lest we assume a person's faith to be precisely the same from one day to the next. Yet the question is not laid to rest. Readers of Smith's work seem still to hear him saying that behind the varied forms of faith there is a common activity of being faithful, which can be understood (perhaps can *only* be understood) *as if* it were the same for a Christian and for a Muslim, for a Hindu or a Jew. (Or a Buddhist? Therein may lie a clue.) Just what the specificable characteristics of that common activity are is one of the as yet (1976) unresolved issues in Smith's writings; his forthcoming book on faith and belief may clarify matters somewhat.

Transcendence and Truth. If we assume faith to be a common denominator, then the specification of its character could rest either on the common humanity of us who have it, or on the entity or being in which it is placed. Although Smith's emphasis on the *activity* of having faith might seem at first to make the discussion of any *object* of faith unnecessary, he has tended to speak of the object of religious faith as "transcendence."

To Smith, transcendence is normally symbolized by the God concept, but not necessarily so. In Theravada Buddhism, the standard borderline-case example of non-theistic faith, Smith finds the *dharma*, the Buddhist "law" (a law both descriptive of the flux of life and prescriptive for man's falling into line with it) to function analogously to the role that "God" fulfills in Western religious traditions.

A test of Smith's understanding of "transcendence" is its application outside the traditions commonly regarded as religious, notably the instance of Marxism. To Smith, the Marxist vision is indeed transcendent; transcendence, it would seem, is not necessarily an eternal transcendence of temporality but is conceivable even if there is no goal beyond history. It may well be that in the future men will find transcendence outside the received religious traditions; but Smith sees such a promise from Marxism as having collapsed with the Soviet Union's dropping of utopian idealism.

The concept of God stands not only as a personal representation of transcendence but as the supreme expression of truth. Implicit in Smith's writing are at least three conceptions of truth, all of which he affirms; for convenience I shall term these existential, moral, and propositional. At first blush Smith may seem to emphasize an existential notion of truth, in that religious traditions become true for their *participants* as they commit themselves to them and experience God through them. But these traditions are also to be seen as morally true by the *observer* in that in the observer's judgment they conform to the will of God.

The status of propositional truth in relation to God is more ambiguous, for Smith has at times pitted morality against doctrine and opted for morality, as in the first essays in this collection. In some discussions philosophers of religion have contended that despite his moral emphasis Smith has not extricated himself from the making of propositional truth-claims. But a trend in some of Smith's later writing, such as the last essay in this anthology, is to view all of man's rational activity as a dedication analogous to religious commitment and to view all truth as deriving from the Truth, that is, God.

The Interplay of Individual and Community. The priority Smith accords to individual faith in contrast to cumulative tradition, and the adjective "personalist" Smith has used to describe his approach, have combined to furnish the impression to some of Smith's readers that he is an individualist, and a typically Protestant one at that. In my view, the situation is not so simple.

The term "personalist" does not imply individual as opposed to corporate, but rather, contrasts with "impersonal" (and with "externalist") in Smith's writing. In characterizing his interpretation of religion as "personalist" Smith intends no school of philosophy but means quite simply that one seeks to understand the faith of persons. In other words, the reality with which the investigator deals is a personal reality, which is why Smith holds in the ninth essay in this collection that objectivity, using techniques established for the study of objects, is conceptually and morally wrong when applied to man.

Although Smith indeed does not emphasize a theological justification or appreciation of the Church as an institution, it would be unfair to proceed to a caricature of each man as alone with God without reference to human community. Communal loyalty or identification, after all, is a factor in virtually every phase of every tradition's history; without community, tradition can hardly exist. But community is more than a topic for description; a truly inclusive sense of community among mankind is a moral obligation. Smith sees it as urgent that religious men in various traditions should strive to make the world a more harmonious place to live in, and insofar as they do they are helping to live up to the potential of their diverse traditions. The agony of intercommunal strife, with Hindu-Muslim massacres attending the partition of India in 1947, was for Smith a searing reminder that men often fall short of the ideal.

Comparative Religion: The Participant's Analysis. It seems so simple and so obvious to say, as Smith has said, that religious faith is the faith of persons, and yet so much of Western description of Asian religion in the nineteenth and early twentieth centuries treated Asian religion unflatteringly, as though no reasonable person could have such faith. A supercilious attitude obtained not only in Christian missionaries' views of Asia, but also in Western Orientalists' interpretations. Its traditions were not portrayed (to use John Clark Archer's title) as "faiths men live by." And nobody seemed to mind. Smith, in his McGill inaugural lecture in 1950, compared such externalist description to flies crawling around on the outside of a goldfish bowl, making detailed observations on the fish inside, but never asking, or finding out, what it feels like to be a goldfish.

Smith's departure from the missionary-and-Orientalist pattern is to contend, first of all, that to speak about another person's religion one must speak *with* that person. The purpose of such conversation is not merely to gain information for one's analysis; it is to validate the interpretation offered of the results. If, for example, I describe Islam, I must do so in such a way that a Muslim can recognize his faith in my description and affirm the description as true. Such a practice is by no means brand new with Smith; various surveys of religion have been submitted informally for approval to members of diverse communities. But Smith formalized the spokesman role in building into the structure of the McGill Institute of Islamic Studies the stipulation of equal numbers of Muslims and of Westerners.

Notice the massive expectation here: the Muslim who serves as the dialogue partner is expected to play two roles simultaneously. On the one hand, he is to be an informant concerning his personal faith and his received tradition, a representative of his community. On the other, he is also supposed to master the methods and materials of Western historical and critical scholarship sufficiently that he can endorse his Western colleagues' descriptions and advance his own academic career by similar contributions. The success of the type of enterprise Smith has advocated depends, in the long run, not merely on maintaining a continuing supply of open-minded, empathetic Western students but on finding Asians who can wear two hats at once, participating in their own classical tradition while at the same time producing Western-style scholarship.

The "Great" Religions. Smith's approach, employing dialogue with the participant as a principal avenue to understanding a religious tradition, manifestly emphasizes the "great," "living," or "world" religions, focusing on those which are numerically or politically significant at the present time. Whereas fifty years ago surveys of man's religious traditions devoted extensive space to prehistoric and ancient religion, much recent interpretation (by no means Smith's work only) has focused on the canonical list of Buddhism, Christianity, Hinduism, Islam, and usually Judaism. What place have the cults of the ancient Egyptians, Babylonians, or Greeks? Curiously enough, less "historical" scholars such as phenomenologists of religion, for whom the widest variety of traditions as sources is of advantage in mapping out constant or recurring patterns of religious symbolism, find religions of the past of more immediate use for their theorizing than does Smith the historian, whose work emphasizes intensive encounter with an individual tradition in preference to across-the-board theorizing. Is Smith then limited exclusively to living traditions? The Norwegian historical scholar Per Kvaerne, writing in the journal *Temenos* in 1973, questioned the appropriateness of Smith's commitment to dialogue as restrictive on this point, and elicited from Smith the rejoinder in the same journal that dialogue may take place across the ages, such as with Smith's "friend" al-Taftazani, who died six centuries ago.

Comparative Religion: The Analyst's Participation. It is not only the Asian partner to the dialogue who must play more than one role. We who study religion in the West also bring multiple commitments to the enterprise. We have noted that the Western intellectual is part of a rationalist, humanist tradition from which the classical ethos of the university as a community of inquiry is derived. Yet we also participate *as religious men* in the enterprise of interreligious understanding. It has characterically been Smith's expectation that people who study Asian religion come from a tradition of their own: that besides being Western academics, they are Methodists or Presbyterians or Unitarians or whatever. Institutionally, this characterized the work of the Center for the Study of World Religions at Harvard, in that it was a program maintained in proximity to the Divinity School, expected to enrich the life of a Christian theological community in ways large and small. At the individual level, Smith expected students in the Harvard program in the study of religion to be passably conversant with the details of "their own" religious tradition as well as specializing in the study of "a religious tradition other than their own."

Very clearly, then, the paradigm of the proper study of religion is not the cold detachment from contemporaneity which marks Orientalist philology, nor for Smith is it the analytic detachment from human community and concern which marks some behavioral-science efforts. Western students enter into an interpersonal and interreligious conversation, best prepared to appreciate someone else's faith and tradition by having a faith and tradition of their own.

So the connections between description and evaluation are many. The reader who now proceeds with this collection will best understand Smith if he listens for Smith to speak to him intellectually, morally, and religiously: with analytic reasoning, but at the same time with deep personal concern.—ED.

PART ONE

Religious Diversity and Truth

1

The Christian in a Religiously Plural World*

Religious diversity is a fact. Not all the religious people in the world are Christians, even to the most wishful of thinkers; and the consequences of a sympathetic or even a realistic view of others for Christian theological positions which would claim a monopoly on truth are devastating. In our times, Smith argues, we have seen the end of the era when Christian theologians could maintain any credibility while ignoring the reality of man's religiousness in such other traditions as the Buddhist and the Islamic.

At times innocently ignorant, at times smug and disdainful, Christian theology has clung to the view that only at the foot of the cross does man find salvation. Within the Christian tradition such a claim has the value of doctrinal truth. This value has been held supreme; if men without Christian faith did not give assent to Christian doctrine, so much the worse for those men.

Smith's strategy is to counter Christian investment in the value of doctrinal truth with another value also central to the Christian tradition: the moral value of acceptance of other men.

* Reprinted in slightly abridged form from Wilfred Cantwell Smith, *The Faith of Other Men* (New York: The New American Library of World Literature, Inc.), pp. 105–128. Copyright © 1963 by Wilfred Cantwell Smith. Used by permission. Now available © 1972 Harper Torchbook Edition.

By this token, to tell the Hindu that he has not found salvation is a very un-Christian thing to do. Nowhere has Smith stated this more compellingly or more engagingly than in this essay.

The essay was first presented as an address to a joint session of the Canadian Theological Society, the Canadian Church History Society, and the Canadian Society of Biblical Studies, meeting in Montreal on May 18, 1961. Smith had previously broached the point that Christian theological isolationism must end in a Canadian Institute on Public Affairs and Canadian Broadcasting Corporation presentation, "The Christian and the Religions of Asia," in 1969, accessible in The Christian Century *under the title "Christianity's Third Great Challenge" (April 27, 1960).*

The influence of Smith's line of argument may be seen for example in a development which took place in 1966, when the General Council of the United Church of Canada issued a document, World Mission: Report of the Commission on World Mission, *containing the statement that God works creatively and redemptively in various religions. That view represents a remarkable and encouraging change from the same denomination's statement of only a few years earlier, cited by Smith in this essay: that without the particular knowledge of God in Jesus Christ, men do not really know God at all.*—ED.

We live, if I may coin a phrase, in a time of transition. The observation is a platitude; but the transitions themselves through which we are moving, the radical transformations in which we find ourselves involved, are far from hackneyed. Rather, there is excitement and at times almost terror in the newness to which all our cherished past is giving way. In area after area we are becoming conscious of being participants in a process, where we thought we were carriers of a pattern.

I wish to attempt to discern and to delineate something at least of the momentous current that, if I mistake not, has begun to flow around and through the Christian Church. It is a current which, although we are only beginning to be aware of it, is about to become a flood that could sweep us quite away unless we can through greatly increased consciousness of its force and direction learn to swim in its special and mighty surge.

I refer to the movement that, had the word "ecumenical" not been appropriated lately to designate rather an internal development within the on-going Church, might well have been called by that name, in its literal meaning of a world-wide humanity. I mean the emergence of a true cosmopolitanism, or according to the wording of my title, the Christian Church in a religiously plural world, which of course is the only world there is. Like the other, *the* "ecumenical" movement, this transformation, too, begins at the frontier, on the mission field, the active confrontation of the Church with mankind's other faiths, other religious traditions. We shall begin there, too, but shall presently see that the issues raised cannot be left out there in the distance. They penetrate back into the scholar's study, and pursue us into what we were brought up to think of as the most intimate and most sanctified recesses of our theological traditions.

Regarding the missionary movement itself, I shall begin by stating quite bluntly and quite vigorously: the missionary enterprise is in profound and fundamental crisis. There has been some temptation to recognize this more on the practical than on the theoretical level. There has been some temptation, perhaps, even not to recognize it at all!—or at least, not to recognize how serious, and how far-reaching, it is: that the whole Church is involved, and not merely "those interested in missions."

At the practical level the situation is acute enough. It is not only in China that the traditional missionary venture has come or is coming to an end. Take the problem of recruitment: more have remarked on the fact that volunteers today are either scarce or curious, than that today no mission board can in fact offer any young person a life vocation on the mission field. Since some persons in the Church at home seem not to realize the kind of feeling on these matters to be found in the non-Western world, I shall quote from the report of a Christian Missionary Activities Enquiry Committee appointed in 1954 by the state government of Madhya Pradesh in India. Among its recommendations were the following:

> Those missionaries whose primary object is proselytization should be asked to withdraw. The large influx of foreign missionaries is undesirable and should be checked. . . .
>
> The use of medical or other professional service as a direct means of making conversions should be prohibited by law. . . .
>
> Any attempt by force or fraud, or threats of illicit means or grants of financial or other aid, or by fraudulent means or promises, or by moral and material assistance, or by taking advantage of any person's inexperience or confidence, or by exploiting any person's necessity, spiritual (mental) weakness or thoughtlessness, or, in general, any attempt or effort (whether successful or not), directly or indirectly to penetrate into the religious conscience of persons (whether of age or underage) of another faith, for the purpose of consciously altering their religious conscience or faith, so as to agree with the ideas or convictions of the proselytizing party should be absolutely prohibited. . . .
>
> An amendment of the Constitution of India may be sought, firstly, to clarify that the right of propagation has been given only to the citizens of India and secondly, that it does not include conversions brought about by force, fraud, or other illicit means.[1]

China, Angola, the Arab world after Suez, this sort of attitude in India, and the like are not simply illustrations of a practical problem. They are symptoms of an intellectual, emotional, and spiritual problem in which Christians are involved. Few Western Christians have any inkling of the involvement of the Church within the object of anti-Westernism, or of the religious involvement of the resurgence in Asia and Africa of other communities. Of this resurgence we see usually only the political or economic facets, because these are the only ones that we can understand. The religious history of mankind is taking as monumental a turn in our century as is the political or economic, if only we could see it. And the upsurge of a vibrant and self-assertive new religious orientation of Buddhists and Hindus and the like evinces a new phase not merely in the history of those particular traditions, but in the history of the whole complex of man's religiousness, of which the Christian is a part, and an increasingly participant part. The traditional relation of the Christian Church to man's other religious traditions has been that of proselytizing evangelism, at least in theory. The end of that phase is the beginning of a new phase, in which the relation of the Church to other faiths will be new. But what it will be, in theory or practice, has yet to be worked out—not by the Church alone, but by the Church in its involvement with these others.

The missionary situation of the Church, then, is in profound crisis, in both practice and theory. The most vivid and most masterly summing up of this crisis is perhaps the brief remark of Canon Max Warren, the judicious and brilliant and sensitive and responsible General Secretary in London of the Church Missionary Society. His obituary on traditional mission policy and practice is in three sentences: "We have marched around alien Jerichos the requisite number of times. We have sounded the trumpets. And the walls have not collapsed."

We come back from the mission field to North America, and to theology. Traditional missions are the exact extrapolation of the traditional theology of the Church. The passing of traditional missions is a supersession of one phase of the Church's traditional theology. The "ecumenical" movements have been the result in part of pressures from the mission field because there the scandal of a divided Christendom came most starkly to light. It is from the mission field also that the scandal of a fundamental fallacy in traditional theology has been shown up.

The rise of science in the nineteenth century induced a revision in Christian theology—what has sometimes been called the second Reformation. Some may think that Canon Warren exaggerates, but at least he calls attention to the seriousness of the new challenge, when he says that the impact of agnostic science will turn out to have been as child's play compared to the challenge to Christian theology of the faith of other men.[2]

The woeful thing is that the meeting of that challenge has hardly seriously begun.

An illuminating story was told me by a Harvard friend, concerning Paul Tillich. Apparently a letter in the student paper, the *Harvard Crimson*, was able to show up as superficial in a particular case this eminent theologian's understanding of religious traditions in Asia. Some would perhaps find it not particularly surprising that an undergraduate these days should know more on this matter than a major Christian thinker. Until recently, certainly, it was not particularly expected that a man should know much, or indeed anything, about the religious life of other communities before he undertook to become a spokesman for his own. To me, however, the incident raises a significant issue. Looking at the matter historically, one may perhaps put it thus: probably Tillich belongs to the last generation of theologians who can formulate their conceptual system as religiously isolationist. The era of religious isolationism is about to be as much at an end as that of political isolationism already is. The pith of Tillich's exposition has to do with its deliberate aptness to the intellectual context in which it appears: the correlation technique, of question and answer. But that context as he sees it is the mental climate of the Western world; and he has spoken to it just at the end of its separatist tradition, just before it is superseded by a new context, a climate modified radically by new breezes, or new storms, blowing in from the other parts of the planet. The new generation of the Church, unless it is content with a ghetto, will live in a cosmopolitan environment, which will make the work of even a Tillich appear parochial.[3]

Ever since the impact of Greek philosophy on the Church, or shall we say the forced discovery of Greek philosophy by the Church, in the early centuries, every Christian theology has been written in the light of it. Whether the Christian thinker rejected or accepted it, modified or enriched it, he formulated his exposition, aware of it, and aware that his readers would read him in the light of it. No serious intellectual statement of the Christian faith since that time has ignored this conceptual context.

Similarly, ever since the rise of science, the forced discovery of science by the Church, again subsequent Christian doctrine has been written in the light of it. Formulator and reader are aware of this context, and no intellectual statement that ignores it can be fully serious.

I suggest that we are about to enter a comparable situation with regard to the other religious traditions of mankind. The time will soon be with us when a theologian who attempts to work out his position unaware that he does so as a member of a world society in which other theologians equally intelligent, equally devout, equally moral, are Hindus, Buddhists, Muslims, and unaware that his readers are likely perhaps to be Buddhists or to have Muslim husbands or Hindu colleagues—such a theologian is as out of date as is one who attempts to construct an intellectual position unaware that Aristotle has thought about the world or that existentialists have raised new orientations, or unaware that the earth is a minor plant in a galaxy that is vast only by terrestrial standards. Philosophy and science have impinged so far on theological thought more effectively than has comparative religion, but this will not last.

It is not my purpose in this essay to suggest the new theological systems that the Church will in the new situation bring forth. My task is to delineate the problems that such a system must answer, to try to analyse the context within which future theological thought will inescapably be set. Intellectually, we have had or are having our Copernican Revolution, but not yet our Newton. By this I mean that we have discovered the facts of our earth's being one of the planets, but have not yet explained them. The pew, if not yet the pulpit, the undergraduate if not yet the seminary professor, have begun to recognize not only that the Christian answers on man's cosmic quality are not the only answers, but even that the Christian questions are not the only questions. The awareness of multiformity is becoming vivid, and compelling.

Before Newton's day it used to be thought that we live in a radically dichotomous universe: there was our earth, where things fell to the ground, and there were the heavens, where things went round in circles. These were two quite different realms, and one did not think of confusing or even much relating

the two. A profoundly significant step was taken when men recognized that the apple and the moon are in much the same kind
of motion. Newton's mind was able to conceive an interpretation
—accepted now by all of us, but revolutionary at the time—that
without altering the fact that on earth things *do* fall to the
ground and in the heavens things *do* go round in circles, yet saw
both these facts as instances of a single kind of behaviour. In the
religious field, the academic approach is similarly restless at the
comparable dichotomy that for each group has in the past seen
our tradition (whichever it be) as faith, other men's behaviour as
superstition, the two realms to be explained in quite unrelated
ways, understood on altogether separate principles. The Christian's faith has come down from God, the Buddhist's goes round
and round in the circles of purely human aspiration, and so on.
The intellectual challenge here is to make coherent sense, in a
rational, integrated manner, of a wide range of apparently comparable and yet conspicuously diverse phenomena. And the academic world is closer to meeting this challenge than some theologians have noticed.

Certain Christians have even made the rather vigorous assertion that the Christian faith is *not* one of "the religions of the
world," that one misunderstands it if one attempts to see it in
those terms. Most students of comparative religion have tended
to pooh-pooh such a claim as unacceptable. I, perhaps surprisingly, take it very seriously indeed; but I have discovered that
the same applies to the other traditions also. The Christian faith
is not to be seen as a religion, one of the religions. But neither is
the faith of Buddhists, Hindus, Muslims, or Andaman Islanders;
and to think of it so is seriously to misunderstand and distort it.
This is a large issue that I have treated in my book *The Meaning
and End of Religion*. I believe there is no question but that
modern inquiry is showing that other men's faith is not so different from ours as we were brought up to suppose.

Religious diversity poses a general human problem because it
disrupts community. It does so with new force in the modern
world because divergent traditions that in the past did and could

develop separately and insouciantly are today face to face; and, perhaps even more important and radical, are for the first time side by side. Different civilizations have in the past either ignored each other or fought each other; very occasionally in tiny ways perhaps they met each other. Today they not only meet but interpenetrate; they meet not only each other, but jointly meet joint problems, and must jointly try to solve them. They must collaborate. Perhaps the single most important challenge that mankind faces in our day is the need to turn our nascent world society into a world community.

This is not easy. Men have yet to learn our new task of living together as partners in a world of religious and cultural plurality. The technological and economic aspects of "one world," of a humanity in process of global integration, are proceeding space, and at the least are receiving the attention of many of our best minds and most influential groups. The political aspects also are under active and constant consideration, even though success here is not so evident, except in the supremely important day-to-day staving off of disaster. The ideological and cultural question of human cohesion, on the other hand, has received little attention, and relatively little progress can be reported, even though in the long run it may prove utterly crucial, and is already basic to much else. Unless men can learn to understand and to be loyal to each other across religious frontiers, unless we can build a world in which people profoundly of different faiths can live together and work together, then the prospects for our planet's future are not bright.

My own view is that the task of constructing even that minimum degree of world fellowship that will be necessary for man to survive at all is far too great to be accomplished on any other than a religious basis. From no other source than his faith, I believe, can man muster the energy, devotion, vision, resolution, the capacity to survive disappointment, that will be necessary— that *are* necessary—for this challenge. Co-operation among men of diverse religion is a moral imperative, even at the lowest level of social and political life.

Some would agree that the world community must have a religious basis, conceding that a lasting and peaceful society cannot be built by a group of men that are ultimately divided religiously, that have come to no mutual understanding; but would go on to hold that this is possible only if their own one tradition prevails. No doubt to some it would seem nice if all men were Roman Catholics, or Communists, or liberal universalists; or if all men would agree that religion does not really matter, or that it should be kept a private affair. Apart, however, from those that find such a vision inherently less appealing, many others will agree that for the moment it seems in any case hardly likely. Co-existence, if not a final truth of man's diversity, would seem at least an immediate necessity, and indeed, an immediate virtue.

If we must have rivalry among the religious communities of earth, might we not for the moment at least rival each other in our determination and capacity to promote reconciliation? Christians, Muslims, and Buddhists each believe that only *they* are able to do this. Rather than arguing this point ideologically, let us strive in a friendly race to see which can implement it most effectively and vigorously in practice—each recognizing that any success of the other is to be applauded, not decried.

We may move from the general human level to the specifically Christian level. Here I have something very special to adduce. It is a thesis that I have been trying to develop, and is essentially this: that the emergence of the new world situation has brought to light a lack of integration in one area of Christian awareness, namely between the moral and the intellectual facets of our relations with our fellow men.

I begin with the affirmation that there are moral as well as conceptual implications of revealed truth. If we take seriously the revelation of God in Christ—if we really mean what we say when we affirm that his life, and his death on the cross, and his final triumph out of the very midst of self-sacrifice, embody the ultimate truth and power and glory of the universe—then two kinds of things follow, two orders of inference. On the moral level, there follows an imperative towards reconciliation, unity, harmony, and brotherhood. At this level, all men are included: we strive to break down barriers, to close up gulfs; we recognize all men as neighbours, as fellows, as sons of the universal father, seeking Him and finding Him, being sought by Him and being found by Him. At this level, we do not become truly Christian until we have reached out towards a community that turns mankind into one total "we."

On the other hand, there is another level, the intellectual, the order of ideas, where it is the business of those of us who are theologians to draw out concepts, to construct doctrines. At this level, the doctrines that Christians have traditionally derived have tended to affirm a Christian exclusivism, a separation between those who believe and those who do not, a division of mankind into a "we" and a "they," a gulf between Christendom and the rest of the world: a gulf profound, ultimate, cosmic.

I shall come to the theological consideration of these theological ideas in the last part of this essay. At the moment, I wish to consider the moral consequences of our theological ideas. Here my submission is that on this front the traditional doctrinal position of the Church has in fact militated against its traditional moral position, and has in fact encouraged Christians to approach other men immorally. Christ has taught us humility, but we have approached them with arrogance.

I do not say this lightly. This charge of arrogance is a serious one. It is my observation over more than twenty years of study of the Orient, and a little now of Africa, that the fundamental flaw of Western civilization in its role in world history is arrogance, and that this has infected also the Christian Church. If you think that I am being reckless or unwarranted here, ask any Jew, or read between the lines of the works of modern African or Asian thinkers.

May I take for illustration a phrase, not unrepresentative, which was under discussion recently by the United Church of Canada's commission on faith, and which ran as follows: "Without the particular knowledge of God in Jesus Christ, men do not really know God at all." Let us leave aside for the moment any question of whether or not this is true. We shall return to that presently. My point here is simply that, in any case, it is arrogant. At least, it becomes arrogant when one carries it out to the non-Western world. In the quiet of the study, it may be possible for the speculative mind to produce this kind of doctrine, provided that one keep it purely bookish. But except at the cost of insensitivity or delinquence, it is morally not possible actually to go out into the world and say to devout, intelligent, fellow human beings: "We are saved and you are damned," or, "We believe that we know God, and we are right; you believe that you know God, and you are totally wrong."

This is intolerable from merely human standards. It is doubly so from Christian ones. Any position that antagonizes and alienates rather than reconciles, that is arrogant rather than humble, that promotes segregation rather than brotherhood, that is unlovely, is *ipso facto* un-Christian.

There is a further point at which the traditional position seems to me morally un-Christian. From the notion that if Christianity is true, then other religions must be false (a notion whose *logic* I shall challenge later), it is possible to go on to the converse proposition: that if anyone else's faith turns out to be valid or adequate, then it would follow that Christianity must be false—a form of logic that has, in fact, driven many from their own faith, and indeed from any faith at all. If one's chances of getting to Heaven—or to use a nowadays more acceptable metaphor, of coming into God's presence—are dependent upon other people's not getting there, then one becomes walled up within the quite intolerable position that the Christian has a vested interest in other men's damnation. It is shocking to admit it, but this actually takes place. When an observer comes back from Asia, or from a study of Asian religious traditions, and reports that, contrary to accepted theory, some Hindus and Buddhists and some Muslims lead a pious and moral life and seem very near to God by any possible standards, so that, so far as one can see, in these particular cases at least faith is as "adequate" as Christian faith, then presumably a Christian should be overjoyed, enthusiastically hopeful that this be true, even though he might be permitted a fear lest it not be so. Instead, I have sometimes witnessed just the opposite: an emotional resistance to the news, men hoping firmly that it is not so, though perhaps with a covert fear that it might be. Whatever the rights and wrongs of the situation theoretically, I submit that practically this is just not Christian, and indeed is not tolerable. It will not do, to have a faith that can be undermined by God's saving one's neighbour; or to be afraid lest other men turn out to be closer to God than one had been led to suppose.

Let us turn, finally, to the theological problem, which the existence of other religious communities poses for the Christian (and that today's new immediate and face-to-face awareness of their existence poses urgently). This problem began, in a compelling form, with the discovery of America, and the concomitant discovery of men on this continent who had been "out of reach of the gospel." In theory the peoples of Africa and Asia could have heard the gospel story and could have believed it and been saved. If they had not become Christian, this could be interpreted as due to their cussedness, or to Christian lethargy in not evangelizing them, and so on. But with the discovery of "redskins" in America who had lived for fifteen centuries since Christ died, unable to be saved through faith in him, many sensitive theologians were bewildered.

In our day a comparable problem is presented, and may be viewed in two ways. First, how does one account, theologically, for the fact of man's religious diversity? This is really as big an issue, almost, as the question of how one accounts theologically for evil—but Christian theologians have been much more conscious of the fact of evil than that of religious pluralism. Another way of viewing it is to phrase a question as to whether or how far or how non-Christians are saved, or know God. The diversity question has got, so far as I know, almost no serious answers of any kind. The latter has found a considerable number of attempted answers, though to my taste none of these is at all satisfactory.

On the former point I would simply like to suggest that from

now on any serious intellectual statement of the Christian faith
must include, if it is to serve its purpose among men, some sort of
doctrine of other religions. We explain the fact that the Milky
Way is there by the doctrine of creation, but how do we explain
the fact that the Bhagavad Gita is there?

This would presumably include also an answer to our second
question. Here I would like merely to comment on one of the
answers that have in fact been given. It is the one that we have
already mentioned: "Without the particular knowledge of God
in Jesus Christ, men do not really know God at all." First, of
course, one must recognize the positive point that this intellectualization stems from and attempts to affirm the basic and
ultimate and of course positive faith of the Church that in Christ
God died for us men and our salvation, that through faith in
him we are saved. In the new formulations to which we may look
forward, this positive faith must be preserved. Yet in the negative
proposition as framed, one may see a number of difficulties, and
one may suppose that the force of these will come to the increasingly felt in coming decades.

First, there is an epistemological difficulty. How could one
possibly know?

If one asks how we know the Christian faith to be true, there
are perhaps two kinds of answer. First, we ourselves find in our
lives, by accepting and interiorizing and attempting to live in
accordance with it, that it proves itself. We know it to be true
because we have lived it. Secondly, one may answer that for now
almost two thousand years the Church has proven it and found it
so—hundreds of millions of people, of all kinds and in all circumstances and in many ages, have staked their lives upon it,
and have found it right. On the other hand, if one is asked how
one knows the faith of people in other traditions to be false, one
is rather stumped.

Most people who make this kind of statement do not in fact
know much about the matter. Actually the only basis on which
their position can and does rest is a logical inference. It seems to
them a theoretical implication of what they themselves consider

to be true, that other peoples' faith *must* be illusory. Personally, I think that this is to put far too much weight on logical implication. There have been innumerable illustrations of man's capacity for starting from some cogent theoretical position and then inferring from it logically something else that at the time seems to him persuasive but that in fact turns out on practical investigation not to hold. It is far too sweeping to condemn the great majority of mankind to lives of utter meaninglessness and perhaps to Hell, simply on the basis of what seems to some individuals the force of logic. Part of what the Western world has been doing for the last four centuries has been learning to get away from this kind of reliance on purely logical structures, totally untested by experience or by any other consideration. The damnation of my neighbour is too weighty a matter to rest on a syllogism.

Secondly, there is the problem of empirical observation. One cannot be anything but tentative here, of course, and inferential. Yet so far as actual observation goes, the evidence would seem overwhelming that in fact individual Buddhists, Hindus, Muslims, and others have known, and do know, God. I personally have friends from these communities whom it seems to me preposterous to think about in any other way. (If we do not have friends among these communities, we should probably refrain from generalizations about them.)

This point, however, presumably need not be laboured. The position set forth has obviously not been based, and does not claim to be based, upon empirical observation. If one insists on holding it, it must be held *against* the evidence of empirical observation. This can be done, as a recent writer has formulated it:

> The Gospel of Jesus Christ comes to us with a built-in prejudgment of all other faiths so that we know in advance of our study what we must ultimately conclude about them. They give meanings to life apart from that which God has given in the biblical story culminating with Jesus Christ, and they organize life outside the covenant community of Jesus Christ. Therefore, devoid of this saving knowledge

and power of God, these faiths not only are unable to bring men to God, they actually lead men away from God and hold them captive from God. This definitive and blanket judgment . . . is not derived from our investigation of the religions but is given in the structure and content of Gospel faith itself.[4]

Again, a careful study by a neo-orthodox trainer of missionaries in Basel, Dr. Emanuel Kellerhals, says that Islam, like other "foreign religions," is a "human attempt to win God for oneself, . . . to catch Him and confine Him on the plane of one's own spiritual life, . . . and for oneself to hold Him fast."[5] He knows this, he says explicitly, not from a study of Islam but before he begins that study, from his Christian premises; he knows it by revelation, and therefore he can disdain all human argument against it. The position seems thoroughly logical, and once one has walled oneself up within it, impregnable. Those of us who, *after* our study of Islam or Indian or Chinese religion, and after our fellowship with Muslims and other personal friends, have come to know that these religious traditions are not that, but are channels through which God Himself comes into touch with these His children—what answer can we give?

One possible answer is that empirical knowledge does in the end have to be reckoned with, does in the end win out even over conviction that claims for itself the self-certification of revelation. We do not deny that upholders of this sort of position are recipients of revelation, genuinely; but we would argue that the revelation itself is not propositional, and that their interpretation of the revelation that they have received is their own, is human and fallible, is partial, and in this case is in some ways wrong.

In fact, we have been through all this before. A hundred years ago the Christian argued that he knew by divine revelation that the earth was but six thousand years old and that evolution did not happen, and therefore any evidence that geologists or biologists might adduce to the contrary need not to be taken seriously. A repentant Church still claims revelation but now admits that its former theology needed revision. In the twentieth century the increasing evidence that the faith of men in other religious communities is not so different from our own as we have traditionally asserted it to be, although it is forcing some to abandon any faith in revelation at all, will in general, we predict, force us, rather, to revise our theological formulations.

Finally, even on the side of internal Christian doctrine the exclusivist position is theoretically difficult. For according to traditional Christian doctrine, there is not only one person in the Trinity, namely Christ, but three persons: God the Father, God the Son, and God the Holy Spirit. Is God not Creator? If so, then is He not to be known—however impartially, distortedly, inadequately—in creation? Is He not active in history? If so, is His spirit totally absent from any history, including even the history of other men's faith?

It may be argued that outside the Chrisitan tradition men may know God in part, but cannot know Him fully. This is undoubtedly valid, but the apparent implications are perhaps precarious. For one may well ask: Is it possible for a Christian to know God fully? I personally do not see what it might mean to say that any man, Christian or other, has a complete knowledge of God. This would certainly be untenable this side of the grave, at the very least? The finite cannot comprehend the infinite.

What does one actually mean when one speaks of the knowledge of God? It has been said, and I think rightly, that the only true atheist is he who loves no one and whom no one loves, who is blind to all beauty and all justice, who knows no truth, and who has lost all hope.

Christians know God only in part. But one part of their knowing Him is the recognition that He does not leave any of us utterly outside His knowledge.

It is easier, however, of course, to demolish a theological position than to construct an alternative one. The fallacy of relentless exclusivism is becoming more obvious than is the right way of reconciling a truly Christian charity and perceptivity with doctrinal adequacy. On this matter I personally have a number of views, but the one about which I feel most strongly is that this matter is important—while the rest of my particular views on it are not necessarily so. In other words, I am much more concerned to stress the fact that the Church must work, and work vigorously, and work on a large scale, in order to construct an adequate doctrine in this realm (which in my view it has never yet elaborated), than I am concerned to push my own particular suggestions. Most of all I would emphasize that whether or not my particular construction seems inadequate, the position formulated above from which I strongly dissent must in any case be seen to be inadequate also.

Having expressed this caution, I may nonetheless make one or two suggestions. First, I rather feel that the final doctrine on this matter may perhaps run along the lines of affirming that a Buddhist who is saved, or a Hindu or a Muslim or whoever, is saved, and is saved only, because God is the kind of God whom Jesus Christ has revealed Him to be. This is not exclusivist; indeed, it coheres, I feel, with the points that I have made above in dissenting from exclusivism. If the Christian revelation were *not* true, then it might be possible to imagine that God would allow Hindus to worship Him or Muslims to obey Him or Buddhists to feel compassionate towards their fellows, without His responding, without His reaching out to hold them in His arms. But because God is what He is, because He is what Christ has shown Him to be, *therefore* other men *do* live in His presence. Also, therefore we (as Christians) know this to be so.

I rather wonder whether the fundamental difficulty in the formulated position, and in all similar statements, does not arise somehow from an anthropocentric emphasis that it surreptitiously implies. To talk of man's knowing God is to move in the realm of thinking of religion as a human quest, and of knowledge of God as something that man attains, or even achieves. Of course it does not state it thus, but it skirts close to implying somehow that we are saved by *our* doings (or knowings). Must one not, rather, take the Christian doctrine of grace more seriously? The question must be more adequately phrased: Does God let Himself be known only to those to whom He has let Himself be known through Christ? Does God love only those who respond to Him in this tradition?

We are not saved by our knowledge; we are not saved by our membership in the Church; we are not saved by anything of *our* doing. We are saved, rather, by the only thing that could possibly save us, the anguish and the love of God. While we have no final way of knowing with assurance how God deals or acts in other men's lives, and therefore cannot make any final pronouncement (such as the formulator of the position stated has attempted to make), nonetheless we must perhaps at least be hesitant in setting boundaries to that anguish and that love.

The God whom we have come to know, so far as we can sense His action, reaches out after all men everywhere, and speaks to all who will listen. Both within and without the Church men listen all too dimly. Yet both within and without the Church, so far as we can see, God does somehow enter into men's hearts.

NOTES

1. As cited in Edmund Perry, *The Gospel in Dispute: The Relation of Christian Faith to Other Missionary Religions* (New York, 1958), pp. 18–19.

2. In an address at Scarborough, Ontario, October 18, 1958.

3. It is pleasant to report that after my remarks were first set forth Dr. Tillich, having spent some time in Japan, published four lectures on *Christianity and the Encounter of the World Religions* (New York, 1963).

4. Perry, *The Gospel in Dispute*, p. 83.

5. Emanuel Kellerhals, *Der Islam: seine Geschichte, seine Lehre, sein Wesen,* 2d ed. (Basel and Stuttgart, 1956), pp. 15–16. Translation by W. C. S.

2

Is the Qur'an the Word of God?*

Fully as stimulating as the declarations Wilfred Smith has made are some of the questions he has asked. Smith delights in the attempt to put matters in a new light by asking whether something taken uncritically for granted was always so, or might ever be otherwise. Smith's investigation of the history of meaning of the term "religion," for example, was hinted at in a lecture given in Princeton in 1957 which bore the never-asked-in-quite-that-way-before title "Is Islam the Name of a Religion?"

In this essay, with the question of whether the Qur'an is the word of God, Smith is asking us less in fact about the form and content of the Qur'an as a text than he is about the presuppositions and precommitments of the investigator who approaches the Qur'an. I would put it as a rule of thumb for the study of religion that "you get out what you put in." If you are ready to see the Qur'an as God's word, much will accrue to you from such a willingness; if you are firmly persuaded that the Qur'an is only man's word, your results will be different.

Smith first presented this essay to a Christian theological audience, as the first in a series of three Taylor Lectures at Yale

* Reprinted in slightly abridged form from Wilfred Cantwell Smith, *Questions of Religious Truth* (New York: Charles Scribner's Sons), pp. 39–62. Copyright © 1967 by Wilfred Cantwell Smith. Used by permission of the publisher.

Divinity School, New Haven, April 16–18, 1963, and subsequently published the lectures under the title Questions of Religious Truth. *In that series he affirmed his characteristic position that religions are not to be thought of as fixed entities which people can "have." Far more important than to "have a religion" as a noun is to "be religious" adjectivally; far more important than to be "a Christian," taking a label, is to be "Christian," exemplifying or striving to exemplify a certain type of life. Religious traditions are not therefore true (or false) as systems of propositions; they* become *true (or are falsified)—not simply to the extent that their adherents live up (or fail to live up) to the traditions, but, more importantly in Smith's view, to the extent that through the traditions they live in accordance with the standard of God, that is, of Truth itself.*

*In doctrine, then, the Qur'an to some is, and to others is not, the word of God. In life and experience, which to Smith are more important than doctrine, the Qur'an has the potential of becoming the word of God.—*ED.

That God speaks, or has spoken, to man has long been a joyous proclamation or quiet assumption of religious faith; more recently, however, it has seemed less clear what such a conviction might mean. I propose that we can illuminate this matter by asking: Is the Qur'an the word of God? This query, I suggest, is worth discussing, is a question that will repay thoughtful consideration for a moment.

First of all, we must observe an arresting fact: that in the past, there have normally been two answers to this question—namely, "yes," and "no." Each of these answers has tended to be clear and straightforward. Some people have given one, some people the other; but whichever it was, it has been given with confident assurance, and even with force. Indeed, for over thirteen centuries now, much of mankind has been divided, quite sharply, into two groups, between whom the boundary has been clear and at times the gulf deep: those that have held that the Qur'an is

the word of God, and those who have held that it is not. Now
this, I submit, is a remarkably curious situation, once one pauses
to reflect on it. Let us elaborate a little on how curious it is.

The question, after all, is not a minor one. If a problem were
peripheral to man's serious concerns, then there would be no
harm, and little cause for comment, if it went unresolved even
for centuries, as this one has. But this question—and others, of
course, not unlike it, but this one will suffice to illustrate for us
the issues that are involved—this question is manifestly radically
important.

Those who have answered it "yes" have taken the answer pas-
sionately. They have been willing to die for it; and what is
perhaps more important, if one remarks that people may be
stirred to die for many roseate causes, they have been willing to
live for it too, to order their lives in accord with it, day after day,
year in, year out, generation after generation, patterning their
behaviour and controlling their choices and selecting their goals,
and to persist, firmly but quietly—against both opposition and
distraction, against both attack and indifference—in taking it
seriously. (Christians are in danger of missing the full force of
the Muslim position on this matter by supposing that the anal-
ogy with the Qur'an is the Bible. Rather, the parallel is to the
Christian doctrine that Jesus Christ is the Word of God.
Throughout this present discussion the point should be borne in
mind that the Muslim attitude to the Qur'an resembles the
Christian attitude to Christ.)

The other group, those whose answer has been "no," have in
one sense shown no corresponding passion or fanfare. Yet their
persistence has been hardly less steady; and the seriousness of
their rejection, not really less. Their conviction has been just as
firmly held that the answer is not only "no," but is obviously
"no"—so obviously "no" that the matter is not worth bothering
about. The West's very indifference to the question is a measure
of the profundity of its assurance. Westerners allowed centuries
to pass without going around busily asking themselves whether
the Qur'an is the word of God, not because they did not have the

time or were unconcerned, not because they thought that such issues did not matter (what could matter more?), but because at heart they took for granted that they knew very well what the answer was.

One may guess that this is still true today for many modern men.

Britain at the turn of this century was fairly persuaded that the Indian rope trick was a fake, but it was not totally sure, and was interested in finding out: eager to explore and willing to be convinced. On the Qur'an, on the other hand, the "no" as well as the "yes" group has been certain of its position at a very deep level indeed.

The question, then, is not a minor one. Nor are the groups that have answered it this way or that. It is no small band of eccentrics that holds this book to be God's word, nor is the idea a passing fashion among some volatile crowd. Those who have held it are to be numbered in the many hundreds of millions. And as we have already remarked, it has continued to be held over wide parts of the world for century after changing century. Civilizations are not easy to construct, or to sustain; yet great civilizations have been raised on the basis of this conviction. Major cultures have sprung from it, winning the allegiance and inspiring the loyalty and shaping the dreams and eliciting the poetry of ages proud to bow before its manifest grandeur and, to them, limpid truth. A thousand years ago the world looked differently from how it looks today; partly, at that time Europe was an underdeveloped area, while the Islamic empires, of whose splendour a caricature has been preserved for our children in the Arabian Nights, were the centre of scientific achievement, of economic might, of military prowess, of artistic creativity—empires built and manned by those who not incidentally but centrally said "yes" to the question that we are considering. On their "yes" they built and held all their achievements.

Equally impressive, however, have been those who have said "no." They, too, are not negligible. They, too, are to be numbered in the hundreds or thousands of millions. They, too, have constructed great civilizations, have made great cultures dynamic. The outsider to Islam distorts his world if he fails to recognize what has been accomplished on earth by those inspired by the positive response. The Muslim distorts *his*, if he fails to appreciate the possibilities evidently open and beckoning to those who say "no."

By this one is not suggesting that the matter is irrelevant. Far from it. To be rejected almost out of hand is any thesis that religious matters are inconsequential in human history; much modern knowledge can be devoted to championing the opposite. The word of God is or ought to be men's crucial concern. And even the secular historian must reckon much more profoundly than has been his recent wont with man's religiousness and its massive expressions. Islamic history cannot begin to be understood if one fails to see it in its fundamentally Islamic quality. That is trite; but one may go on to say, perhaps a little more provocatively, that European history cannot really be understood either unless its underlying "no" to the Islamic question is taken into account. At certain points this is obvious—Charles Martel at the battle of Poitiers, the Crusades, Lepanto, the siege of Vienna, and so on—but it is true also at many others. The only reason an historian can write the history of Europe without tracing throughout the fact of its resounding or tacit "no" to our question is the simple reason that he takes that "no" so utterly for granted, and presumes so unconsciously that his readers will take it for granted also. Few will dispute the contention that the history not only of the Muslim world but of Christendom would have been seriously different from what it has been, had our question been answered differently on either side.

The two groups, then, have been numerous, prodigiously numerous. And they have been great, of monumental influence. They have also (and here we approach the heart of our problem) been intelligent. At least, they have included intelligent men, highly intelligent. There have been stupid and petty persons, no doubt, on both sides, and human history would have been different without them. Yet among those who said "yes" to our question, and among those who said "no" to it, there have been men of keen, indeed of superlative, intelligence. Each answer has been sustained by persons brilliant, wise, informed, careful, honest, critical, and sincere. It is sometimes said that people simply accept the religious beliefs with which they are brought up. Yet even if this were true of ninety-nine per cent of a community, it would be in a sense quite defensible and hardly worth comment if the other one per cent, the leaders whom the followers accept, are independent thinkers.

Perhaps what I have been saying will sound platitudinous. We all know that people differ on religious questions, so why the fuss? This brings us to a further matter: that we men have not only given two opposite answers to this question, but we have also come to accept such a fact without disquiet. This is curious. The radical divergence might well make both groups more restless with their own answers than either has often thought it necessary to be. At the very least, there is an intellectual challenge: how is one to rationalize the divergence, to conceptualize it, to interpret it intelligibly? Are our minds to be content to accept lying down the total divergence, unreconciled, on a major issue?

This acceptance, as a matter of fact, is a little more complicated than might appear. It does exist, on both sides. Yet on both sides, it appears on inquiry, there are certain tendencies toward qualifying it. This is not surprising, since to accept the dichotomy on the intellectual level, fully, is to set for oneself a quite serious theoretical problem; and it is easier, certainly more comfortable, to suppress or evade such problems than to solve them. This can be done among the negative group, the non-Muslims, by not recognizing the intelligence to be found on the other side. If one does not know, or does not appreciate, this, then it becomes possible to dismiss the other position as "superstition"— that is, as ideas that are held without any grounding in reason, and that are not a serious option for the enlightened.

This stand has, in fact, often been taken, either openly or surreptitiously, consciously and disdainfully or subtly and unawares.

On the Muslim side something similar occurs. There there is

also a further, rather subtler rejection. Some Muslims seriously
believe that the prophethood of Muhammad—that is, the belief
that the Qur'an comes through him from God—is so rational and
straightforward as to be self-evident; so that anyone who rejects
it is obtuse or perverse, or both. This idea underlies a good deal
of the bitter Muslim reaction to the Western academic study of
Islamics. Another Muslim stand questions not the intelligence
but the moral integrity of the "no" group. It supposes that the
non-Muslim recognizes the theoretical validity of the Qur'an's
being from God but that he nonetheless, for reasons best known
to himself (or to God), chooses not to "submit" to it, not to live
in accord with its message. I have actually met Muslims who
believed this; and who felt that this view paid the Christian the
compliment of presuming that he was not so stupid or so spiritually insensitive or so discourteous as to be blind to the Qur'an's
authenticity, and accepted him as a strange character who chose
not to live up to the vision that had been vouchsafed him. I
sometimes wonder if this attitude, conscious or unconscious, on
the part of Muslims is perhaps more widespread than one
imagines.

However that may be, and however many persons there may be
on either side who have not recognized the situation in its true
starkness, my own position, quite firmly, is that one must accept,
what is empirically the case, both intelligence and sincerity on
both sides. A hidden disdain for the other party is a psychologically perhaps satisfying but morally reprehensible and intellectually untenable refuge. Our problem rests on facts, and must
be dealt with as such. To the question, "Is the Qur'an the word
of God?" some men, intelligent and sincere, say "yes," and some
men, also intelligent, also sincere, say "no."

If we explore this matter somewhat further, an additional re-
finement becomes necessary—one of great importance. For in
actual practice, though the answers have indeed been given, the
question has not really been asked. By this I mean that the
question, though it logically precedes the answers, historically
follows them. It is presupposed, but not formulated. And indeed

is not a religious *Weltanschauung* largely a matter of presuppositions? The professional task of academic comparative religionists
is to intellectualize, if possible, what is going on in the religious
life of the great communities of mankind. Our business is precisely to bring into the open in theoretical formulation the positions that men of faith inwardly take, and particularly to bring
into the open the questions to which their religious positions are
the answer. In most cases, of course, this is a very much more
exacting and subtle affair than in the present one. Sometimes it
takes years of patient exploration, and great depths of sensitive
understanding, to discern what those questions are. Yet even in
the present case, where the question is quite straightforward and
obvious, nonetheless in practice it has hardly ever been asked.
This fact too can be illuminating.

In the Muslim world, you will not find, or would not have
found for centuries gone by, a lecture announced for theologians
carrying as its title the question with which we have begun this
essay. Nor do I know of any book in the Muslim world with this
title. Muslims do not publicly ask, "Is the Qur'an the word of
God?" There are many books, and no doubt there have been
many lectures, in which the answer (the affirmative answer) has
been given. But there are not books, and have not been lectures,
in which the question was asked, precisely because the answer
was given, was known, was accepted. Perhaps it was not firmly
accepted, and had to be argued, or explained, buttressed or con-
firmed. Hence the books. Hence the long debates among the
theological schools, the long explanations and discriminations,
the interpretations of meaning, the ferreting out of subtleties,
the long history of theological discussion and conflict. Yet the
whole discussion and debate, with all its ramifications, comes
under the heading of answer, not under the heading of question.

Similarly in the West. Without looking into the matter, one
may guess that it was probably novel that a lecture by a Christian minister in a Christian theological setting should bear the
title, "Is the Qur'an the Word of God?" as happened when the
draft of this essay was first given in the Taylor Lectures at Yale

Divinity School. Again, the reason is the same: the question has not been asked, because the answer has been constant. One may suppose that anyone who undertook to go through previous Taylor Lecture series at Yale would find the answer "no" to our question given many, many times; and certainly in other theological seminaries, and other activities of Christendom over the centuries, the answer "no" has been reiterated endlessly. We said at the beginning that we would ask that this question be considered seriously; in asking this, it appears, one is asking not only something perhaps novel, but even something searching, something radical. Indeed, one of the profound movements of our time, of which the leaders of the Church are restlessly and uncomfortably aware, is that the Church, inchoately but disturbingly, is beginning to ask this kind of question, not rhetorically, but genuinely. It is beginning to ask it because it is beginning to feel, inchoately but disturbingly, that the long-standing answers may not be adequate, or at least that they are not self-evident.

The Muslim world, also, is moving into what may possibly become a profound crisis, too, in that it also is just beginning to ask this question instead of being content only with answering it. Young people in Lahore and Cairo, labour leaders in Jakarta and Istanbul, are beginning to ask their religious thinkers, and beginning to ask themselves, "Is the Qur'an the word of God?" Answering this question has been the business of the Muslim world for over thirteen centuries. Asking it is a different matter altogether, haunting and ominous.

In fact, the question, "Is the Qur'an the word of God?" insofar as it is a genuine question, is a threat—both to Christian and to Muslim theology, simultaneously and for the same reason.

A Christian theologian who asks it would be probably at least a heretic, if that category of thought were still in use. A Muslim who asked it publicly today might quite possibly be killed.

Before we explore this explosive matter, however—the dynamics of modernity, the transformation through which we are living, or on which at least we are embarked—there remains one major point about the past positions, the answers. Each side has tended to think of the other as prejudiced. If one removes the pejorative flavour of that accusation, there is a certain validity on both sides, in the technical sense that each position is in fact a "pre-judgment," a coming to the problem with one's mind already made up. Muslims do not read the Qur'an and conclude that it is divine; rather, they believe that it is divine, and then they read it. This makes a great deal of difference, and I urge upon Christian or secular students of the Qur'an that if they wish to understand it as a religious document, they must approach it in this spirit. If an outsider picks up the book and goes through it even asking himself, "What is there here that has led Muslims to suppose this from God?" he will miss the reverberating impact. If, on the other hand, he picks up the book and asks himself, "What would these sentences convey to me if I believed them to be God's word?" then he can much more effectively understand what has been happening these many centuries in the Muslim world.

It is not only Christian theologians or missionaries, however, whose answer has been a taken-for-granted "no." The Western academic scholar, too, has not studied the Qur'an asking himself whether this be divine or human. He has presumed before he started that it was human, and he has studied it in that light. Some of the more sensitive outside scholars have remembered, as they studied, that *Muslims* believe this to be God's word; others have done not even that, one would judge from their writing; but virtually none of them, quite manifestly, has ever asked himself, "Is God speaking to me in these words?" I said just now that I doubt whether Christian ministers have in the past lectured to ministers under a title, "Is the Qur'an the Word of God?" I am quite confident that no academic scholar in the West has ever lectured on this theme. For one may be sure that the question has never occurred to him to be needing asking. If you scrutinize the scholarly studies of such Western students of the Qur'an as Arthur Jeffery, Richard Bell, Régis Blachère, and the others, you will realize that such a possibility never once entered their minds. They did not conclude that the Qur'an is the word of Muhammad; they started with that view, which was never for a moment challenged. In the last century this was formulated in so many words (unwittingly, of course; the writer was simply dealing with the question of whether the text now available is historically reliable): "We hold the Kor'ān to be as surely Mohammad's word, as the Mohammadans hold it to be the word of God."[1]

Both the "yes" and the "no" positions, then, are pre-convictions.

Further—and this is major—both positions work. Each has found a pragmatic justification. Those who adopt either position, and follow it through consistently, find their reward. Perhaps there is in the end no more cogent argument for any religious position, Christian or other, than that those who adopt it find that it authenticates itself. "Our fathers have lived by it over the centuries, and it has proven itself to them; we have tried it ourselves, and we find that it is true." Those who have held the Qur'an to be the word of God have, by holding this, found that God does in fact speak to them through it. They have ordered their lives in accord with it, and have found that that pattern rewards them by bringing them into the divine presence. The Book promises to those who submit to its letter and spirit, guidance and boldness and inner peace and endurance in this world, and felicity in the next. We have no evidence on affairs in the next world, but so far as this world is concerned the promise, to those who believe, has in fact been redeemed. Islamic history, and the godliness of my personal Muslim friends, corroborate the Muslim's affirmative answer.

Equally striking, the outsider's negative answer is also self-authenticating. Western scholars, such as those that I have mentioned, and many others, approach the Qur'an quite heedless of a possibility that it might be God's word; persuaded that its source was mundane, they look for that source in the psychology of Muhammad, in the environment in which he lived, in the historical tradition that he inherited, in the socio-economic-cultural milieu of his hearers. They look for it, and they find it. They find it, because quite evidently it is there. Muslims may protest all they like that such scholars are dishonest; the fact is that they are human, and like all scholars they may and do make mistakes, and like all scholars they admit it, and yet essentially they have been motivated by intellectual integrity, by scientific method, by dis-interested, disciplined inquiry. Where their hypotheses have failed to explain the facts, they have changed the hypotheses, or at least the next generation has. Not only does the method work; it has proven enormously fruitful. Western scholarship on the Qur'an has uncovered a mass of material otherwise quite lost: has reconstructed an historical picture, has traced developments, has established interpretations, that are unassailable.

Those who hold the Qur'an to be the word of God have found that this conviction leads them to a knowledge of God. Those who hold it to be the word of Muhammad have found that this conviction leads them to a knowledge of Muhammad. Each regards the other as blind. From what I have said, you will perhaps discern that in this matter I feel that in fact each is right.

So much for the past. In a schematically simplified way I have delineated the situation that has arisen over the centuries as men have adopted one or the other of two essentially dogmatic and contradictory answers to our question. I have hinted that at the present time in this matter, as in every other in which man is involved, change is beginning to be discernible. And for the future, I am prepared to speculate that something quite new in this realm both will and should develop—new not only in content but in form.

In the past the two answers to our question, "yes" and "no," have been both personal and social; but even in the personal case, they have tended to be not individualist, but in groups. A whole community has given one answer, and a whole community the other. The two groups have then lived in isolation from each other, in basic ignorance of each other. And such contact as there has been between the two has more often than not been conflict —suppressed, in rivalry and disdain, or overt, in war. From now

on, one may devoutly hope that the violence at least, and presently the conflict and even the disdain, have been or may be left
behind. And the isolation and ignorance are in process of depart-
ing, from both sides. Civilizations in the past lived insouciant of
each other; this is no longer so, and clearly, for the future, we
shall be living in "one world." We have become aware of each
other, quite vividly; and are gradually becoming aware of each
other at a cultural and even a theological level, so that our lives
from now on are to be lived in a global society in which all of us
are intermingling participants.

So far as our particular problem goes, this means that the days
are surely over when we can be content with a situation in which
some of us, either glibly or emphatically, give one, and others of
us give another, of two stridently different answers to what has
appeared to both of us to be a relatively straightforward, and
certainly an important, question. At least, I for one am simply
restless at so conspicuously irrational a dichotomy. As an intellectual, I feel challenged by the theoretical incoherence; I feel
driven to strive for an answer that, if it has not yet attained
universal validity, will at least have transcended the evident limitations of the dichotomized past.

Of course, another possible reaction to the discomfort of an
intolerable contradiction is not on the intellectual level but on a
practical: to seek a solution not by finding a new answer intellectually that will do justice to the facts of the present polarity,
but by striving to create a new situation, in which the dichotomy
will have been replaced by a uniformity. On the Muslim side,
this moral response takes the form of missions. The Islamic has
been one of the three or four great missionary movements on our
planet. Throughout Islamic history there have been those unwilling to accept a world divided into those that answered "yes"
and those that answered "no," who therefore set out to convert
the others, so that all would say "yes." In the other direction, a
counterpart is a possible debunking mission, aimed at discourag-
ing any "yes" answer. We may note that in the past this debunking has been common both to Western secularists and to Chris-

tians, the latter having taken for granted that to affirm Christ as the word of God "of course" involves saying "no" to the Qur'an's being the word of God too.

We shall return to this point later; at the moment I would simply remark that it does not seem likely that the intellectual problem will be solved for us in this missionary way—in either direction—by changing the status quo so radically that the question will no longer arise.

I do not know how many will share my sense of an intellectualist imperative to construct a theoretical answer more comprehensive, coherent, and unifying than the traditional ones. Quite apart from that, anyway, there are certain contemporary historical considerations to which one must attend. These indicate that whether we like it or not—new types of answer, new analyses of the question, are in fact being engendered. These considerations are directly related to the point that we have just made: that the isolation of the two groups is giving way to an intermingling, and the ignorance of each for the other is giving way to awareness.

I have argued that each of the two groups' answers does, in fact, work. This is true on its own premises, and within the confines of its own group. One may rephrase the situation more accurately, by saying that each *has* worked, for its own group, so long as the isolation of that group from the other has been maintained. Now that that isolation is disappearing, however, both the pragmatic and the theoretical justification of each answer are proving inadequate.

Let us take the "no" answer first, as it has been worked out carefully by Western Orientalist scholarship. That answer, we have said, has shown itself capable of accounting for all the facts about the Qur'an—except the facts of the religious life of the Muslim community, the life that has developed since, among those who have said "yes" to our question. Western scholarship on the Qur'an has taken the Qur'an as a seventh-century-Arabian document and, as such, has analysed and explained it roundly. It has not much considered it, however, and has not much ex-

plained it, as an eighth- and a twelfth- and a twentieth-century
document, as a continuingly contemporary and timeless book on
which the faith of men of faith has been continuingly fed. It has
studied it as a literary document, and has brilliantly understood
it as a literary document. It has done little to understand it, or
even to try to understand it, as a religious document: living, life-
giving, the point at which the eternal not only is thought to, but
for a devout Muslim actually does, break through into time,
lifting him out of his historical environment and introducing
him, not only in theory but in exuberant practice, to transcendence. How the Qur'an came to be what it is, is one question, to
which the Western skeptic has addressed himself. How the
Qur'an came to do what it has done, for believing Muslims across
the centuries since, is another: the actual life-giving source of the
religious life of the continuing community.

As this latter is becoming more known, as contact has grown
with living Muslims as men of faith, as knowledge and insight
have increased not only into the outward facts of Islamic history
but into the inward life of those who have lived within that
history as servants of a living and speaking God; so the awareness
has come that the traditional Western answer explains only some
of the phenomena. It is true insofar as it goes, but it has become
increasingly evident that it does not go far enough.

We said above that scientific inquiry stands ever ready to mod-
ify its hypothesis; and as a matter of fact, the non-Muslim West
has just begun to soften, even to withdraw, its "no." In one of his
later articles the professor of Arabic at Harvard, Sir Hamilton
Gibb, doyen of Western Islamicists, explicitly states in passing:
"For myself, I unhesitatingly accept the term 'Revelation' (in
Arabic *tanzil*, "sending down" or *waḥy*, "inner communication")
as the description of Muḥammad's personal experience, although
Islam, like the other monotheistic religions, is faced with the
necessity of reinterpreting the no longer tenable mediaeval concepts of 'revelation'."[2]

Similarly, a Christian theologian like Kenneth Cragg, leading
theorist of Protestant missions to Muslims, no longer responds to

the Qur'an by rejecting it theologically.[3] And it seems clear that the next generation of scholars, without accepting the traditional Muslim answer, will go beyond the traditional non-Muslim one. What answer they will give is not yet evident, not even to them; so that it is not too fanciful to suggest that the non-Muslim observer of Islam is for the first time engaged in asking the question that we are discussing. He is in the midst of a search, for a new type of answer: neither a simple "yes" nor a simple "no" but some *tertium quid*, more subtle, more complex, tentative, yet to be hammered out.

Similar considerations pertain for the Muslim world, for the group that has traditionally answered a straightforward "yes." This answer, too, has worked; it has proved richly rewarding, fruitful, creative. It has justified itself. Yet it too has worked within its own premises, and has justified itself within a community isolated in large part from others. Just as the "no" answer has served satisfactorily to explain the Qur'an itself, but not to explain the facts to which the "yes" answer has given rise, so in reverse the "yes" answer of the Muslims has served to cope with the Qur'an itself, but it does not cope with the facts to which the "no" answer has given rise. The Muslims' affirmative answer, or the elaborations of it that the community has developed, have been able to handle the matters that have arisen within the community. But in our day it has been proving itself incapable of handling the new historical data that Western scholarship on the Qur'an, for example, has been not only uncovering but making available also to Muslims. The knowledge, the reconstructions, that skeptical historical criticism from abroad has purveyed, makes the traditional "yes" answer, in its traditional form, inadequate.

Until now, the situation has been rather desperately complicated by political overtones: Western scholarship has been resisted, or decried, by Muslims as a tool of Western imperialism, as something deliberately calculated to undermine Muslims' faith; malicious, and, it was hoped, irrelevant. Yet even those who do not feel that Western imperialism is a horse too dead to be worth flogging any more, are not immune from a new emergence. For this non-Muslim scholarship is being taken up these days not only by the infidel West, but by Hindus in India and Buddhists in Japan, and to some degree even by the new generation of Muslims themselves. Isolationism is going; in principle, it is gone. Like the rest of us, Muslims from now on are going to have to live their lives, even their religious lives, as participant members of a world community.

The historical facts that give sense to the proposition that the Qur'an is a mundane product, can no more be gainsaid by Muslims than can, by outside observers, the religious facts that give sense to the proposition that it is a divine word, a power of God unto salvation for those that believe.

And although much of the Muslim world is on the defensive against what seems to it the attacks and threats of outside theories, nonetheless the best minds and most honest spirits in that community are themselves sincerely searching for a new answer to our question, one that will do equal justice to the transcendent element in their tradition, and yet will at the same time be meaningful and persuasive to those whose horizon is global and whose historical understanding is realistic. As a modernist Pakistani has shown in a revealing study, the answers of acute minds in classical Islamic terms themselves to our question were not so simplicist as more recent conceptions would suggest.[4] A Muslim friend told me once that his wife was startled to learn (from him) that the Qur'an did not "come down" to Muhammad from heaven as a bound volume; another Muslim friend once told me that, for him, the Qur'an was the word of God to Muhammad just as the *Messiah* was "revealed" to Handel, who said of it that the heavens were opened to him and he heard this music and wrote it down.

In other words, the Muslim world also is beginning to be in search of an answer to our question more subtle, more realistic, more historical, more complex than the traditional "yes" or "no."

Significant in this new situation, where both traditional groups are setting out in search of a larger answer, is the novel develop-

ment that to an unprecedented extent they are beginning to
deliberate on each other's books. Symbolic of the end of isolation
are the new collaborative academic centres that are being set up,
in which Western scholars and Muslims work together toward
understanding, so that every remark about Islam by a Westerner
is consciously made in the presence of Muslims, and every remark
about Islam by a Muslim is explicitly made in the presence of
those who cannot give a simple "yes" to our question.

Perhaps because I believe seriously in the unity of knowledge,
and believe seriously in the unity of mankind, I rather imagine
that the only answer to our question that will satisfy the non-
Muslim and the only answer that will satisfy the Muslim will in
coming years have to be identical. I am not unaware that this is a
radical position, crucial for Christian theology and also for Islamic. That it is radical does not disturb me, since I am deeply
persuaded that in the twentieth and twenty-first centuries the
religious history of mankind will be taking a major turn. Yet
that Christian theology must, and I think will, ponder this question, and hammer out some answer for itself, is both an illustration and a measure of the newness of not only Christian life, but
of Muslim life as well. I cannot see how in principle any answer
to our question can be truly adequate for a Christian unless it
were also and simultaneously truly adequate for a Muslim; and
yet if that be true, how profoundly novel the religious history of
both our groups has become!

I do not mean that Christians and Muslims will cease to be
different; but I do suggest that intellectually their understand-
ings must converge, even if morally they choose to respond differently. Reactions to the universe, the existential religious response,
may presumably continue to be a personal or group adventure.
Theory, on the other hand, it is the business of those of us who
are intellectuals to universalize.

I have elsewhere elaborated the thesis that the task of comparative religion is that of constructing statements that will be
true in more than one tradition simultaneously. Even if one does
not wish to follow me here, nonetheless the minimum fact that

from now on Christian theologians will be professionally at work on a central issue of Islamic theology (and perhaps presently also vice versa) will make it not only true, but vivid, that a new age in man's religious development is being ushered in.

We live, then, in a world where for all men a question such as that with which we began is becomimg an open question, to which the answer is not known but has to be discovered, and where the question itself is no longer simple but has to be understood. One may at a minimum suggest that we do not yet know fully all the ways in which God has spoken, and speaks, to man.

NOTES

1. William Muir, *The Life of Mohammad from Original Sources*, ed. T. H. Weir (Edinburgh, 1912), p. xxviii, quoting without precise reference "Von Hammer," presumably Joseph von Hammer-Purgstall.

2. Hamilton A. R. Gibb, "Pre-Islamic Monotheism in Arabia," *Harvard Theological Review* 55 (1962): 269.

3. See, for instance, his *The Call of the Minaret* (London and New York, 1956) and *Sandals at the Mosque* (London and New York, 1959).

4. Fazlur Rahman, *Prophecy in Islam* (London and New York, 1956).

3

The Study of Religion and the Study of the Bible*

In the sixteenth century, Biblical authority provided the Protestant Reformers the leverage they needed to counter the institutional authority of the Roman Church. But during the lifetimes of people born since 1900, in the view of some Protestant scholars, Biblical authority has disintegrated under our very eyes.

One important factor that has brought this about has been the historical and literary criticism of the Bible, which treated it as though it were just like any other work of ancient literature. It required a major reorientation in Western thought to bring this about: to remove the Bible from its pedestal of uniqueness and analyze it in terms of historical circumstances and literary genres. That analysis constitutes one of the truly major intellectual accomplishments of the nineteenth century. Men figured out for the first time how both the Old and the New Testament books (particularly the initial collections of each, the Pentateuch and the Gospels) came to take the form in which they would be received by later generations. As Smith observes, such activity focused on cultural and literary influences on the Bible, rather than cultural and literary influences of the Bible.

* Reprinted with minor alterations from *Journal of the American Academy of Religion* 39 (1971) 131–140. Copyright by the American Academy of Religion. Used by permission.

*The remarkable thing is that modern historical analysis of the
Bible, antithetical as it is to certain traditional notions of revelation, should have come to be incorporated into much of twentieth-century Christianity's understanding of itself. In most
major denominations the formal training of the clergy treats the
Bible as part of ancient Near Eastern and Hellenistic history.
Christianity's intellectual leadership speaks of "origins," with all
that that implies for the Bible's world being different from our
own. Such a view of history, which Smith calls backward-looking,
works to the detriment of appreciating the subsequent process of
development in the role of scripture, let alone appreciating the
"timeless" quality of such a mode of expression as myth. How
can we assess the religious truth of myth or of parable if we are
committed to a view of truth and of history which excludes such
narratives from consideration? To the extent that modern man
understands the Bible by supplying its historical context, he cuts
himself off from understanding the piety of two millennia of
Christians—and of Jews—who approached it without the modern historian's sophistication.*

*Smith's challenge to religion scholarship, to focus on the Bi-
ble's function as scripture, has not (as of 1975) been answered in
terms of an observable shift in scripture curricula. What he is
looking for, he expects, will in the long run be offered not by
conventional scripture scholars at all but by historians of religion. And though, in Smith's contention, modern scripture
scholarship has been doing illegitimately limited history, the historical enterprise can yet be put on the right footing. Smith is too
much an historian for history itself to be the villain of the
piece.—*ED.

One of the most exciting new developments on college and university campuses in recent times, and also one of the most significant and potentially creative developments on the religious
scene, is surely the emergence and flourishing of liberal-arts departments of religion. Perhaps what is happening can be summed

up most pithily by saying that the transition has been from the teaching of religion to the study of religion. Where men used to instruct, they now inquire. They once attempted to impart what they themselves knew, and what they hoped (of late, with decreasing expectation) to make interesting; now, on the contrary, they inquire, into something that both for them and for their students is incontrovertibly interesting, but is something that they do not quite understand.

Part of the excitement and potential significance derives from the fact that, for the first time in many long years, with the setting up of religion departments a number of very bright, very concerned young men and women find themselves enabled to throw themselves with vigour and thoroughness into a serious wrestling with religious issues, intellectually, with no prior commitment as to where they will come out in the end. At one time the Church offered the only full-time employment for an intellectual with religious interests, or a religious man with primarily intellectual interests. This worked well, classically, so long as the concept "God" signified, intellectually and emotionally, reality and truth; later, when a commitment to truth began to be felt and seen as different (or perhaps different) from a Christian commitment, fewer and fewer took up (or could take up) the challenge. Now that appointments in religion departments are available, highly promising, highly intelligent, highly serious young people are once again able to devote themselves unreservedly to the task of searching for understanding, knowledge, and integrity in the religio-intellectual field.

The transition from the seminary to the liberal arts department, as the locus of inquiry, has been marked conspicuously by a change, then, in emphasis and form and mood, but less conspicuously than some would like by a change in content. The traditional seminary divisions of the subject matter, or "disciplines," still characterize the religion department more thoroughly than many wish. The salient upsurge of the study of Asian religious life is an obvious exception. One may be allowed to wonder, however, whether both student and faculty eagerness

in "History of Religion"—usually signifying the history of religious groups other than one's own—is altogether related to the
novel content, or whether it is in substantial part a function of
the new mood and method, orientation and attitude, that are
brought to bear in these new studies and are felt to be missing
from the old. Does the popularity of the study of Asia religiously
stem, at least in part, from the fact that those who study it are
able to approach it with today's interest, today's questions, today's moods and methods? The study of Christian data still seems
bound within questions, moods, methods of an earlier era.

Let us take the field of Bible as an illustration. If I were
chairman of a religion department, I would certainly wish to
have in the curriculum a course on the Bible, and on the faculty
a man competent to teach it. What kind of course and what kind
of teacher, however, would I be looking for?

The courses actually available, and the training of men actually available to teach them, are on the whole calculated to turn
a fundamentalist into a liberal. Often they can do this with great
skill, but it is hardly any more a relevant task. The more advanced or sophisticated Biblicists have moved beyond this, to the
point where they are competent historians of the religious life of
the ancient Near East or of the first-century Eastern Mediter-
ranean world. This is fine, for that small group who happen to
be interested in the religious history of those particular sectors of
the total religious history of mankind; but these men seem on the
whole little equipped to answer a question as to why one should
be especially interested in those particular times and places,
rather than in, let us say, classical India or mediaeval China or
modern America.

The sort of course and the sort of teacher for whom I would be
looking in the field of Bible would be different. Let me attempt
to delineate what, as I see it, might fruitfully be attempted.

The course that I envisage would be concerned with the Bible
as scripture. It would begin with some consideration of scripture
as a generic phenomenon. The questions to which it would address itself would be questions such as these: What is involved in

taking a certain body of literature, separating it off from all other, and giving it sacrosanct status? What is involved psychologically; what, sociologically; and what, historically? How and where did it first come about? How did the Christian Church happen to take up this practice? And—once this is done—what consequences follow? One would wish a brief but perhaps striking comparativist introduction: the concept and role of scripture in other major communities—Jewish, Hindu, Buddhist, and the like. Salient differences, as well as striking similarities, could be touched briefly. (For example, the thesis could be considered that in the Islamic system the Qur'an fulfills a function comparable to the role played in the Christian pattern, rather, by the person of Jesus Christ while a closer counterpart to Christian scriptures are the Islamic Hadith ["Traditions"].) The role of formalized and sacralized oral tradition in some societies, as distinct from both written scripture, on the one hand, and ordinary colloquial discourse, on the other, might also be broached. The religious significance of the introduction of writing into human history would be touched upon, perhaps. The basic issue would be: scripture as a religious form.

All this, however, would be introductory only. The bulk of the course would be historical: an investigation into the history of the Bible over the past twenty centuries. Before one considers this with any specificity, the prime point is to recognize that in this fashion the Bible would be treated as a living force in the life of the Church. My own field is Islamics; and in that field I devote a fair amount of time and energy to trying to make vivid to my students the fact that the Qur'an, if it is to be understood in anything remotely approaching its religious significance, must be seen as not merely a seventh-century-Arabian document (which has tended to be the way in which Western Orientalists, as distinct from religionists, have treated it) but also as an eighth-, and a twelfth-, and a seventeenth-, and a twentieth-century document, and one intimately intertwined in the life not only of Arabia but also of East Africa and Indonesia. For the Qur'an has played a role—formative, dominating, liberating, spectacular—

in the lives of millions of people, philosophers and peasants, politicians and merchants and housewives, saints and sinners, in Baghdad and Cordoba and Agra, in the Soviet Union since the Communist revolution, and so on. That role is worth discerning and pondering. The attempt to understand the Qur'an is to understand how it has fired the imagination, and inspired the poetry, and formulated the inhibitions, and guided the ecstasies, and teased the intellects, and ordered the family relations and the legal chicaneries, and nurtured the piety, of hundreds of millions of people in widely diverse climes and over a series of radically divergent centuries.

To study the Qur'an, then, is to study much more than its text, and much more of social conditions than those that *preceded* (or accompanied) its appearance in history and contributed to its formation. The important history for an understanding of this scripture *as scripture* is not only of its background but also, and perhaps especially, of its almost incredible on-going career since. What produced the Qur'an is an interesting and legitimate question, but a secondary one; less minor, less antiquarian, religiously much more significant, is the marvelous question, What has the Qur'an produced? Indeed, any interest that the former question may have is derivative from the power of some at least tacit answer to the latter. It is because of what the Qur'an has been doing, mightily and continuingly, in the lives of men for all these centuries *after* it was launched, that anyone takes the trouble to notice its launching at all. For religious life, the story of formative centuries is logically subordinate to that of subsequent ages. (It is possible to overlook this fact only from within faith; that is, only when the significance for the later period is taken as given.)

The Qur'an is significant not primarily because of what historically went into it but because of what historically has come out of it; what it has done to men's lives, and what men have done to it and with it and through it. The Qur'an is significant because it has shown itself capable of serving men as a form through which they have been able (have been enabled) to deal with the problems of their lives, to confront creatively a series of varied contexts. To understand the Qur'an is to understand both that, and how, this has been happening.

One may go further and ask: What kind of being is man, that he can take such a book (one that outsiders often do not even find interesting) and, having made it a scripture for himself, can go out into the world and in terms of it build a community and a civilization, produce literature and art and law and commercial structures, and in terms of it continue to find meaning and courage in life when the civilization wanes, and nobility in death when life wanes?

He is a feeble and sorry historian who underestimates—under-perceives—the power of symbols in human life, or the power of a scripture to function symbolically and as an organized battery of symbols.

To return to the Christian Bible. It has not played in Western or Christian life the central role that the Qur'an has played in Islamic life; yet the query, what significance *has* it had, is clearly no mean question.

The first point, then, is to see the Bible not merely as a set of ancient documents or even as a first- and second-century product but as a third-century and twelfth-century and nineteenth-century and contemporary agent. Since I myself am an historian, I suppose that my evident predilection is to treat this historically, and to feel that in no other way can its significance be understood. As already suggested, however, I feel that its role (and indeed the role of anything else) in history can be illuminated, and even must be illuminated, by light thrown on human history by psychological, sociological, and comparativist perspectives. The dominant point in this case is to understand the potential and the actual roles of such a scripture in the life of the imagination, its role as an organizer of ideas, images, and emotions, as an activating symbol.

The analytic mode that for some time has dominated Western intellectual life, particularly academic life, tends to take anything that exists and to break it down into parts. Historians too have become victims of this, even at times to the point of failing to recognize that the first business of any historian is to be astonished that any given thing in the historical stream does exist and to try to understand how it came together and what its coming together subsequently meant. If something has been important, we must analyse not only it but also its importance; its history, almost, is the history of its importance. The analysis of a thing is interesting, and can be highly significant, but only subsidiarily; strictly, the history of that thing *begins* once its parts are synthesized. The historian's task is to study the process of synthesis, plus the subsequent process of that synthesis as it moves through later history.

There has developed a tendency, one might almost say, to "study history backwards," as though the task of the historian vis-à-vis any phenomenon in the course of man's story were to observe it and bit by bit to analyse its component parts and causes and antecedents, and to trace them farther and farther back into more and more remote antiquity. Does the historian need reminding that time's arrow is pointed the other way? That the history of a thing is, rather, its ongoing life, its ramifying results, its development and growth and change, eventually perhaps its disappearance or disintegration (forwards) into parts or its transmutation into something else? By all means let us, with regard to anything, know how it became; but let us study further how and what it went on becoming. The study of history must be in large part the study of creativity.

The first imperative for the student of the Bible, accordingly, in the modern world, is not to take the Bible for granted and then to see what it says or what constituent elements went into it, or anything of that kind; but rather, to explain how it came about as a *scripture*, how it came to be that the various elements that comprise it were put together, and how it came about that Christians continued, century after century, to find reason to go on prizing and sacralizing it and responding to it—and with what results.

One minor illustration. Marcion used to be regarded as a

"heretic," and he has been studied as a man who wished to "leave out" the Old Testament from the Bible. This presupposes a two-Testament Bible, instead of being astounded by it. It is possible to take Marcion, rather, as an illustration of the fact that we cannot take for granted that the Christian Bible should be in two parts (let alone exist at all), that it should subsume the Jewish Bible by a device that simultaneously incorporates and supersedes it, and so on. Involved here is the subtle question of the relationship between two religious systems or communities: one could touch briefly here on the somewhat comparable, somewhat different, Islamic handling of both Christian and Jewish positions, as things once valid but now superseded, and on the general issue of how a religious *Weltanschauung* can cope with another community that is historically prior to it in time, but may prove incapable of coping with one that arises subsequently. It would be going too far afield to explore this issue at any length, but any treatment of the Christian Bible that failed to deal with it at least seriously, if briefly, could hardly be considered adequate. The fact that the Jewish Bible is called (and not merely called: rather, is perceived as) the "Old Testament" in Christendom (and still in the Harvard Ph.D. program!) has had profound consequences both in Christian history and in Jewish history (through Christian-Jewish relations).

(A comparativist aside. The history of the Jewish Bible, despite the similarity of text, would constitute a different course—or a separate sector of the Bible as scripture. The fact that the same material has functioned, of course differently, in the lives of two different communities over the centuries could itself be educative, and exciting. How differently, it would be the business of such a study to unfold. That the story of the Exodus served—mightily—as a symbol [activating, salvific?] of liberation for Jews in a way perhaps comparable to that of the Resurrection for Christians could be explored. And so on. But I leave all this aside.)

The fact having been considered, then, that the Christian Church decided (consciously or unconsciously) to have a scripture, and constructively determined that it should have this particular one, the story just begins. The history of scriptural interpretation has been a traditional study (it is even a sub-rubric, or optional extra, in the general examinations of some present Bible doctorates); but this is only a small part of the issue that is now raised. The interpretation ("hermeneutics") of the Bible, and even a study of that interpretation, *presupposes* that a Bible exists and even presupposes that it is (or has been thought) worth interpreting—presupposes without comment the very things that are most fascinating and have been most decisive.

The question is not merely, given a scripture, how the Church exegeted it at various stages; but also, what roles that scripture played, what difference the fact that the Church had one made in the life of the Catacombists, in the intellectualizing of the Fathers, in the reactions of Christians at Rome in the time of the barbarian devastations, and so on. What was the significance of a Bible in the Dark Ages, when exceedingly few people could read? And in the High Middle Ages, for scholastic theology and for Gothic cathedrals and the religious orders? In the life of the imagination in mediaeval times, did the vignettes of incidents from the life of Jesus impinge on the consciousness of Europe through biblical passages, directly, or through stained-glass windows? Later, how did the Bible function in shaping the mystical imagination and the poetry of St. John of the Cross?

For a study of the Bible and its role in the religious life of man, the Reformation obviously signifies a massive new development. (Most Biblical studies for the past hundred years in our seminaries and academic institutions have been studies from within that transition, rather than studies about it. They have assumed that the Bible has the status and the importance that the Reformation gave to it, rather than scrutinizing and interpreting to us that status and importance. It is from this assumption, for instance, that current Biblical scholarship and its doctoral programs arise and therein fail to see, even today, that for the subsequent West, it is the Bible that has made ancient Palestine significant, not vice versa.) What the new post-Reformation

role for the Bible did to people, to their imaginations, to their
perception of the world, to their sexual life, to their domination
of a new continent in America, are such matters that, if one does
not understand them, surely one does not understand the Bible.

Along with the Reformation as—of course—a major factor of
historical change in the role of the Bible in Christendom, and
along with a wide range of other large and small factors operative at about the same time, another clearly major factor was the
invention and widespread use of printing. Our envisaged course
would examine what happened to the role of the Bible in personal and social life when it was not only translated into the
vernaculars but was also multiplied mechanically by type-print.
(The relation of printing to scripture is not straightforward,
however. In Christendom, the Bible was virtually the first thing
to be printed, and was foremost in Western man's response to the
medium; in the Islamic world, on the other hand, when printing
was introduced it was agreed that secular books might be printed
but the Qur'an deliberately was not.)

Closely linked with the question of printing, whose historical
impact on the Bible has, of course, been complex, the spread of
literacy has also been of major impingement. We may take one
colorful example of this matter from life on this American continent, where among some of us tales from the pioneering days of
homesteaders are part of the living lore with which we grew up.
In some families the time is not altogether remote when the
Bible was perhaps the *only book* in a given home. It was trea-
sured and reverenced in a way to which the fact that it was the
only book in the home is surely hardly irrelevant. Clearly that
situation is radically different from a modern home where the
number of books is overwhelming. Our culture has gone through
an intermediate phase in which a good library was a matter of
pride and dignity, even of prestige; a library which certainly
included the Bible, probably as an outstanding item. Nowadays,
in contrast, the number of books pouring off our presses is
inundatingly vast; a collection of books is a burden for which the
apartment-housewife hardly knows how to find space; and in this

situation the role of a scripture—no matter what its content might be, nor what one's faith—can hardly be the same as it was in that pioneering homestead context.

One need not agree with Marshall McLuhan that the age of the printed book, the Gutenberg era, is over, to recognize that with the astronomic number of new books being published every year the age of a very special book, treated differently from all others psychologically, metaphysically, sociologically, is changed.

The more standardly recognized change in Western man's and the Church's understanding of the Bible over the past century has been that effected by the rise of historical criticism. Again, most recent Biblical study has been produced from within that movement. The undergraduate course that we are envisaging here would, rather, look at that movement from the outside: would describe it, analyse it, assess it. The movement, effectively, is over. It can no longer dominate, nor even serve, our understanding of the Bible. Rather, almost vice-versa, it becomes instead part of the nineteenth- and early twentieth-century history of Christian handling of scripture. Clearly a great motif in any modern study of the Bible as scripture would be an inquiry into what happened to it as scripture with the rise, struggle, triumph of historical criticism, and what happened to the local congregation, to the individual Christian, to personal piety, to the Sunday service.

One of the questions that an historical study of the development of the Bible in religious life would profitably tackle, I have long felt, is its role in the bifurcation in Western cultural and intellectual life between myth and history. We are beginning now to apprehend the historical as one form of human consciousness, and to see that form arising historically, recently. Now that we are beginning also, and still more recently, to have a deep and potentially authentic, although still incipient, understanding of the role of myth in human life and society, we can apprehend much more significantly what was happening when the Bible functioned mythically. We have not yet had much serious study of the historical process by which this function has become disintegrated in modern times. To carry it out would require religious scholarship and brilliant sensitivity; but it would be enormously rewarding.

With the relatively recent rise in Western consciousness, culminating in the nineteenth and early twentieth centuries, of the new sense of history, and the (consequent?) careful and rigorous distinction between history and myth, something major happened. One might put the matter this way. Previously—certainly all through the Middle Ages, the early Reformation stage, and among pious Christians right up until the twentieth century— the Biblical stories functioned simultaneously as both myth and history. When a sharp discrimination between these two was pressed in Western intellectual life, what happened by and large was that the West opted for history and rejected myth. This was true even of the Church, which when it had to choose decided to treat the Bible historically. (An heroic choice? And a fateful one. It speaks well for the integrity and courage of the Church's leaders that they chose relentlessly to pursue what they thought to be truth, in this dilemma; but it speaks for their lack of creative discernment, that they, like their contemporaries, thought that history had to do with truth but myth did not.)

Might one almost make symbolic of this development, the moment in the eighteenth century when Bishop Ussher's date 4004 B.C. was bestowed on the first chapter of Genesis? Later, the Church agonized over the fact that that date for creation was wrong. We may recognize now that the problem was not that particular date, but any date at all, the giving of a date; the notion that one is dealing here with historical time, rather than mythical time. (More exactly: this *became* a problem. For there was an earlier time when it was not so, a time before Europe had discovered that myths do not have dates.) If instead Bishop Ussher had used, and editions of the Bible had put in the margins or at the top of the page, the phrase *in illo tempore*, would our history over the past while have been different?

Probably not, because only now are we beginning to apprehend intellectually or self-consciously what kind of realm it is,

what dimension of our life, to which that phrase, or "once upon
a time," refers. When a mediaeval peasant went to church and
saw in a stained-glass window or heard in a sermon an incident
from the life of Jesus, he did not apprehend that incident as
something that happened historically in *our* modern sense of history. Rather, his appreciation was a complex one, in which the
counterpart factors to what we today would regard as the mythical were, I should guess, at least as substantial as those counterpart to our modern sense of literal chronological history.
Through the sacraments and much else, but also because he lived
before the separation between myth and history, Christ was a
present reality in his life—in a way that has ceased to be the case
for most modern men, at the end of a process of demythologiza-
tion the course of which a modern student of the Bible ought to
be able to trace for us. The impetus to demythologize, and the
price that our culture has paid for this and for its inability to
remythologize, are matters that it is the business of a religion
department to study and to elucidate. (Rudolf Bultmann is to
be studied in relation not to the first century so much as to the
twentieth; just as Julius Wellhausen was once interesting for an
interpretation of the second and first millennia B.C., but now for
the nineteenth century A.D.)

Myth and history can be re-integrated by the modern intellect,
perhaps, by pondering the role of myth in human history. The
course that we propose would be no less rigorously historical than
the most austere of historiographies; but it would be the history
of myth that would be illuminated, or better, the historical functioning of myth, the history of man with myth (and more
recently—aberrantly?—without it?). An historical study of the
Bible, to be done well, would inherently have to be an attempt
(typical, some would contend, of a religion department's task in
general) to understand human history as the drama of man's
living his life in history while being conscious of living it in a
context transcending history. The mythical, far from contrasting
any longer with the historical, can nowadays be seen as what has
made human history human. Even those who do not see this,

must recognize that the mythical has in substantial part made human history what it has in fact been. Certainly the history of the West is in significant degree a history of the role of the Bible. Our task, important and exhilarating, is to elucidate this.

Most illuminating of all to elucidate, would be how the Bible has served, and for many still serves, spiritually: What is the meaning of the (historical) fact that through it men have found commitment, liberation, transcendence? In it over the centuries have come into focus for its readers human destiny and all men's ultimate concerns. At certain historical moments it has given both shape and power to men's drive—or call—to social justice; at other moments, to their capacity—or gift—to endure tyranny and terror. It is a scripture in that it deals, has dealt, so far as the actual lives of persons and groups are concerned, only second-arily with finite things and primarily with infinite; here has been given form man's sense of living—in terror, fascination, mystery, and grace—in relation to what is more than mundane, in himself and beyond. Through the Bible men have found not merely ancient history but present salvation, not merely Jesus but Christ, not merely literature but God, millions attest. Those who do not use or understand these terms must wrestle with the fact that multitudes of men have through the Bible been involved with that to which they give such names. To study the Bible must be to strive to understand it as a channel, which it has observably been, between man and transcendence. The Bible has not itself transformed lives, but has introduced men to that which transforms, its committed readers affirm, the historical observer reports, and the department of religion must note and interpret.

The final sector of our course would deal with the question, What does the Church, what does modern man, do with the Bible now? Now that we know and understand that the material that constitutes the Bible is what the historical critics tell us, what next? Now that we have some sophisticated awareness of the role of scriptures in various kinds of culture, of the role of symbols in various kinds of psychology and society, of the role of

myth in human consciousness, what next? Now that we have seen
what the Bible has been in man's life in the past, what shall it be
now? This part of the course could be descriptive and analytic, a
study of the process of what has recently been and is now happening. It could also, in the case of some scholars and teachers of
a possibly creative quality, be constructive.

The role of the Bible in contemporary Christian life—in personal piety, in liturgy, in theological normativeness, in much
else—would be an inquiry continuous with a study of the dynamic role of the Bible in the life of the Church, and of Western
society, over the past many centuries, as well as instructive in
itself.

What the Bible has been, has done, what role it has played in
human life; and what it is doing in modern life, what role it is
playing; and in a few cases where imaginative extrapolation is
allowed, what it may become, what role it may or might or
should yet play in our lives—these are significant questions,
which a religion department might surely tackle, both legitimately and rewardingly. The relation of the Bible to Palestine,
one is almost tempted to say, we might leave to the Orientalist
departments. From religion departments we look for some study,
I would hope historical, of the relation of the Bible to us.

If I were chairman of such a department, I would very deeply
desire to have a course among the departmental offerings on the
History of the Bible as Scripture. Yet where could I find a man
with doctoral training equipping him in this field?

PART TWO

Religious Diversity
and Modernity

4

Traditional Religions and Modern Culture*

With this essay and the two that follow, we focus on the subject of change in religion, particularly on changes taking place as the historical process continues at the present moment.

"Essences, by nature, do not change. I am suggesting that a science of religion can be founded on the observable fact that religions, in history, do change." The quotation is from Wilfred Smith's McGill inaugural lecture of 1949, and deserves repetition as a point fundamental to his approach to religion. "Tradition" may be understood as the cumulative and still changing result of changes carried over from the past; "modernity" is more elusive in this essay because its meaning is assumed rather than stated, but it certainly entails as one of its features a disinclination to accept without question religious forms received from the past.

In his 1963 book The Meaning and End of Religion, *Smith proposes abandoning certain uses of the noun "religion," namely, its application to a particular religious tradition as "a religion" or to more than one as "religions." Such usage tends to "reify,"*

* Reprinted in slightly abridged form from *Proceedings of the XIth International Congress of the International Association for the History of Religions* (Leiden: E. J. Brill, 1968), vol. 1, pp. 55–72. Copyright by E. J. Brill. Used by permission.

*to make static entities out of ongoing, developing traditions. And
while "cumulative tradition," as Smith terms it, is externally
observable, it is not the inner reality of religion. That reality,
expressed variously in various traditions, Smith terms "faith."
Note that while traditions may be many, faith is taken to be
basically one, though without a thorough attempt on Smith's
part in the book to demonstrate its universality.*

While the over-all argument of The Meaning and End of Religion *cannot be easily represented by any one portion extracted
from it, I see the present remarks, prepared two years later, as a
serviceable introduction to Smith's views on the nature of "traditions" particularly in relation to "faith." Thus the tradition/
faith contrast, more than the tradition/modernity of the title,
constitutes Smith's own agenda here.*

*This essay was first delivered on September 9, 1965, in Clare-
mont, California, to a plenary session of the eleventh congress of
the International Association for the History of Religions, the
international professional organization in this comparative field.
The agenda for that program, as is evident from Smith's opening
paragraphs, was tradition/modernity; and Smith's discussion of
the title assigned him is characteristic of his concern to pin down
what's in a name, to note the unstated assumptions which may
underlie terminology casually taken for granted.—*ED.

To define at all accurately what it is that we are being asked to
discuss, is in some way to decide (whether consciously or otherwise) what kind of thing is actually going on religiously in the
contemporary world. At issue is not only the title of the sessions
in which these remarks are delivered, but the general question as
to what is the task of the historian of religion in studying the
particular period of human history that is currently in process.

Let us look, then, at the titles proposed. The one that I accepted, rather innocently as it turned out, was "Traditional
Religions and Modern Culture." I shall have more to say about
it presently. Another version of our topic, as enunciated in the
bulletin, reads, "Traditional Religion under Modern Culture."[1]

The word "under" in that case is surely significant. If one stresses it, as I should tend to do, it would seem to assert, and unstressed it goes even further by apparently taking for granted, that religion is "under" culture. This notion itself can be interpreted in various ways; I suggest that all of them raise questions. One is the sense made popular by a certain type of anthropologist, in whose ideology culture is final, is the ultimate human category, with religion as an element within it and subordinate to it. Or again, this might be taken in the sense of that secularist whose not inquiring mind is already made up that religion, though it may have been dominate or constructive in the past, even generative of culture, yet in modern times has certainly lost the initiative and is in process also of losing the battle. We might almost be thought of as being invited to watch religion going under. This latter type might not speak of "Hinduism under Mauryan culture," or "Islam under Mughul culture," or "Christianity under mediaeval culture," yet subordinates all to modern culture.

Still another wording in one of our bulletins read, "Traditional religion under the impact of cultural modernization."[2] Now this crystallizes a common variant view, which deserves more critical scrutiny than it normally gets. In my study of the Islamic and of the Indian scenes I have had occasion to challenge this view: namely, that modernity is somehow an entity that from the outside delivers a blow of which Islam or Hinduism is the victim. It is worth considering some implications of, and some alternatives to, such a view.

The impact theory has been widely held, usually without argument, perhaps especially by Western administrators, by political scientists, and by economic-aid men. It thinks in terms of a religion as something more or less given, a compact entity inherited from the past in a particular form, and thinks of modernization also as something given, if not in a fixed form at least as a process with a more or less fixed direction, usually imposed or at least illustrated by the recent West. Within this polarity, this view envisages the latter, modern culture, which is dynamic, as actively raining blows on the former, the religion, which is thus at least the recipient, if not simply the victim, of external pressure. The impact idea often seems to suggest a somewhat massive assault under the force of which the traditional system in this dichotomy is seen as reeling, bewildered, if not knocked down.

Now we can all think of particular facts, both in our own personal lives and in contemporary Afro-Asia, that would seem to justify such an interpretation, so that the impact metaphor as a first approximation is not silly. Yet I find it inadequate, and in some ways wrong.

For one thing, thinking of the impact of one thing upon another seems altogether too externalist. Is it not in danger of distorting by minimizing the interiorization of modernity in the religious life of all communities?—an interiorization such that whatever effect there may be takes place not only from the outside but from within. Other metaphors, accordingly, would be needed to supplement this: one might think, for instance, in terms of percolation, or of digestion, or of an artesian well, or of a contagious disease. The impact metaphor also seems to suffer from a serious underestimate of the dynamic, fluid quality of the so-called traditional religious systems. They, too, are in flux; they have their own evolution, which today is in full swing. If one is going to think in dichotomies at all, the proper picture is more nearly the confluence of two rivers than the impact of one rushing river on a rock (or mud) citadel.

The important point, of course, is to keep ourselves reminded that all these, including "impact," *are* metaphors, and only that. My own studies, particularly in the Islamic case but also more tentatively of certain developments in contemporary India, have given me occasion to challenge the impact notion as potentially quite seriously misleading for an authentic understanding of the contemporary Muslim and Hindu scenes, at any but a superficial level.

It is our professional business to inquire into what is going on, not to assume *a priori* any one particular analysis of contemporary religious developments. Hence my contention that it could be profitable to consider these titles themselves in the light of the actual situation, and not vice versa. Particularly in a study of a major civilization other than one's own, and most of all, of the religious life of the men of that civilization, one must learn not to set out seeking answers to questions that one has formulated previously. One must learn, rather—slowly, perceptively, painfully, creatively—to ask new questions, to discern new categories, to sense new visions.

The anthropologists themselves have begun to recognize that there is a dynamic within, and not merely upon, present-day religious life in the Orient. The economic historians and economic planners have swung around to seeing that religion is not simply a deadweight intrusive interference from the past in an otherwise straightforward secular advance, but is potentially a contributor to development, perhaps even of some illusive *sine qua non*—a quality that they do not understand but that they ask us to elucidate for them. Historians of religion can hardly rest content to concentrate on the obvious and traditional while they leave to others or leave unexplored the pioneering and consequential and exciting realms of contemporary religious dynamic.

Alongside the "impact" and "under" titles, there was the more non-committal one presented personally to me, "Traditional Religion *and* Modern Culture." This would seem, at first, comprehensive enough. Maybe if I admit to being restless even with this, seeking to prune away its preconceptions and to break through to a truer wrestling with our subject-matter, and seek to carry you with me into an exploration of newer and more subtle and more fruitful realms, maybe you will turn restive. "Why so fastidious?" you may ask. "Why all this fuss about phrasing? We wish to know what is happening to man's religious life in its various forms in our rapidly innovating modern world. However one may choose one's wording, surely we all know in general what is under discussion."

I must beg forgiveness for my stubbornness; but I am unable to agree that of course we all know what is being discussed, under this heading. My hope is that by considering the inadequacy of its formulations to the current scene we can arrive at a

truer apprehension of this latter, the actual goal of our en-
deavours.

In fact, I feel that one of the most important requirements of
our study is a recognition that we do not quite know what it is
that we are observing—so that our first task is to struggle to find
out. Creativity is required here.

I have hoped to carry you with me not only in my contention
that the relations between religious life and the rest of culture
are to be understood in terms of complex interaction and mutual
involvement, rather than of a one-way impact. I hoped to carry
you with me also in my suggestion that they are relations between religious life "and the rest of culture," and not between it
"and culture" *simpliciter*. The point is important. The latter
dichotomy is Western: our civilization derives its religious tradition from Palestine, its culture from Greece and Rome. It not
only conceptualizes, but institutionalizes, the two separately.
And it has reified the one (as I have shown in *The Meaning and
End of Religion*) but not the other. "Traditional religion and
modern culture" is, accordingly, a Western concept. And to some
extent also it is a Western phenomenon. Of the other civilizations of the world, China has had a formally comparable duality,
with its acceptance and elaboration of a Buddhist movement
from India, but the duality is not one of religion *versus* culture.
Neither is Japan's. India, on the other hand, and the Islamic
world (except in Indonesia) have had a formally more coherent
complex. In contrast with the West, therefore, for Asia—at least
for the Islamic and Indian worlds, and I would advocate a use of
the term "religious" such that this would hold also for the rest of
Asia and for Africa—for the non-Western world, the religious
traditions are the only traditions there are.

(Put differently: "Hinduism" is a modern Western concept
which formulates in Western-cultural terms what can more accurately or only be characterized as Hindu culture, perhaps better as Indian culture.)

In making such generalizations I have in mind such facts as
that the first use of the word *islami* in Arabic was to designate

those Arabic poets who lived subsequent to Muhammad's mission, including Christian poets, and that as late as the nineteenth century, Muslims in India called themselves "Hindu" because they lived in India as Indians. I also have in mind such a situation as the *santri* traditions of Indonesia, which are partly Muslim and partly Hindu; and I would contend that the situation in Java is more aptly understood and more authentically apprehended under my sweeping over-simplification that all the cultural traditions of Asia are religious traditions, than they can be under the standard Western over-simplification that dichotomizes such a situation, into two sets of elements, "religious" and "cultural."

I admit, as you see, that "all the cultural traditions that Asia has are religious traditions" is an over-simplification. Yet I put it forth quite seriously, admitting cheerfully that of course it needs to be refined, yet insisting nonetheless that first it needs to be understood. What I am really suggesting is that a Western student who starts from it is far less likely to make mistakes than is one who starts from a religion-*versus*-culture duality. In fact, he will quite possibly make no mistakes at all; since the exceptions, of which there are many, will be relatively easy to ferret out, if they do not strike him at once, whereas the exceptions to the dichotomizing prejudgment are exceedingly subtle and have escaped many quite erudite scholars.

Of course, another way of saying exactly the same thing is that in non-Western societies there is no such thing as religion: there is only culture. This is what the sociologist Werner Cohn has said—and while I do not suggest that one should necessarily agree with him, I do suggest that it is of the utmost importance that one understand him. To see Asians as not having a religion, only a culture, can be richly illuminating. What one has to grasp, in that case, is the way in which the culture has transcendent overtones.

The really serious complication, of course, is that the important Westernizing élite of Afro-Asia has adopted Western conceptual orientations, to the point where it itself affirms our dichotomy; so that some English-speaking Muslims and Hindus themselves think of traditional religion and modern culture, thereby both confusing Western observers and cutting themselves off in interesting ways from the rest of their own societies, as well as confusing themselves. These élites are indeed important; and this innovation of theirs is not merely a conceptual one. It too is *both* religious and cultural, for good or ill. The history of Pakistan since 1947 illuminates this point richly. The great matter here is that, for political-socio-economic-internationalist reasons, the reification of religion is an historical process, which though very recent in Asia is yet powerful. I have proposed the curious-sounding thesis that Hinduism emerged in the late nineteenth century, and is still in process of coming into being. In the case of Islam I have documented conceptual reification; in the Hindu case it is sociological as well. At the moment let me simply make my point this way: that the emergence of Hinduism and Islam as "traditional religions" is itself a symptom of modern culture.

The existence of a religious phenomenon deriving from the past, and existing in the present as something distinct from and to some extent in conflict with what I have called the rest of culture, is a modern-cultural phenomenon. The historian of religion can study its recent rise, and can analyse the radical innovation in the religious history of the communities concerned that it is in process of constituting. Curiously, this modern-cultural phenomenon of something called "traditional religions" turns out to be not only not traditional, but also not religious, except in quite limited ways. Insofar as there actually has come to be a dichotomy between religion and culture, this particular phenomenon is on the cultural side of that dichotomy, not on the religious side.

This brings us, then, to the other of the two main concepts in our title. If the concept "modern culture" is misleading because it suggests a culture from which religious matters are somehow distinct, the phrase "traditional religion" is misleading for a whole series of reasons. In *The Meaning and End of Religion* I have set forth the reasons that lead me to be dissatisfied with the concept "a religion" and its plural. To think of it as "traditional" reduplicates the fallacy.

For any man whose faith is vivid, even whose faith is at all alive, there are two qualities of that faith (of "his religion," if you insist) that stand out, so far as questions of temporality are concerned: first, that it is timeless; second, that it is present. If religion is anything at all, it is something that links the present moment to eternity. Not to understand this is to have no feel for religious life at all.

I made these statements not as a would-be philosopher of religion, but as an historian of religion. These are historical observations. They might equally well, or better, be cast in this historical form: that if religion has been anything at all, it has been something that linked each succeeding present moment to eternity. In the Hindu case, the lack of concern with historical development that has prevailed until quite modern times, is notorious. The outlook of Muslims, in contrast, has been historical —but not historicist. The difference is of the utmost consequence.

One cannot read the documents of century after century of Islamic religious history with any sensitivity and imagination, without recognizing that they indicate primarily a contemporary reality to those involved. Until at least the late nineteenth century, the Islam of Muslims was a living truth, something that existed primarily in their own day and in their own lives, even though they knew, and were quite interested in, the fact that earlier generations had known it also in theirs; since Muhammad, and in a sense since Adam. The law that a devout Muslim practised was a living reality, was a system of commands that God was enjoining on him, was addressing to him, right then and there, where he stood. That the content of the commands was X rather than Y, he might learn historically; but the force of the command was contemporary, was fresh each morning as he got out of bed.

You will note that I speak of the law that he "practised." He did not obey the law; that is a modern aberration. He practised the law; it was God that he obeyed. The difference is subtle, but profound; and it ramifies. It is one of the many differences between "traditional religion" and religion traditionally. The modern idea of obeying a religious law is part of the havoc that the concept of a traditional religion has wrought and is wreaking.

Similarly for the society of which he was a member. It too was Islamic as a contemporary, living reality. It was so not because it conformed to some abstract pattern deriving from the past (it did not), but was Islamic because it was the scene of his and his neighbours' corporately living out, or failing to live out, their divinely ordained duty. They did not strive to construct an Islamic society; they strove to obey God, and what we (and perhaps they) call an Islamic society resulted.

The same is of course true for Jews, equally historical, equally un-historicist. The covenant was a living covenant of God with every generation of Jews, including one's own. It had had, no doubt, a past event as an historical reference point, but one lived in that covenant as a contemporary reality.

In both cases it was the present reality of faith that gave meaning to history, rather than vice versa. This same truth in the Buddhist case led to the Mahayana glorification of the transcendent, and therefore contemporary, Buddha; and even among Theravadins it was the permanent, timeless, and altogether contemporary *dhamma* and all that it signified and could lead to, that sustained the faithful. The historical Buddha was important any given morning because he had made known once in the past that timeless truth whose relevance and charm and power were at work that particular morning. His significance in the past derived from a living truth of today, rather than the other way around. In every community the living contemporary faith of the adherents has been the cause and not merely the result of the "religion's" history. Ultimately, Hindus do not believe a doctrine because it is part of Hinduism; rather, it is part of what we have come to call Hinduism, because they believe it.

As I said in 1950, before I learned to refine the concept "religion," "all religions are new religions, every morning." One might almost go on to say, the concept "traditional religion" is a contradiction in terms. A man is not religious if his religion is only traditional—or even primarily traditional. There are groups for whom history, even historical tradition, has been religiously important; but only if, and insofar as, and because, it could introduce the devotee to something beyond history, something here and now, and/or beyond all time.

Let no one imagine that the question of what is happening to Islam in Pakistan is anything other than the question of what is happening to man in Pakistan. And even this does not mean only, what is happening to Pakistanis in Pakistan: it is, rather, what is happening to mankind in Pakistan. Let no one imagine that the question of the cow in India is anything less than the question of how we men are to understand ourselves and our place in the universe. The Buddhist's involvement in politics in Vietnam is a political question but also a question of our relation to eternity—yours and mine as well as his. Every time a person anywhere makes a religious decision, at stake is the final destiny and meaning of the human race.

If we do not see this, and cannot make our public see it, then whatever else we may be, we are not historians of religion.

The religious condition of Asia (like that of the West itself) is without any question in process of being radically modified in the twentieth century, largely as a result of the spread throughout the world of a dynamic movement originating in the West by which man is transforming mundane life. What I am contending is that this radical modification is much too complex and dynamic, much too profound and tumultuous, to be described in Western and simplicist terms as the interplay of two factors, one religious (and traditional religious at that), one cultural (and modern culture, at that). Rather, the whole religious (and indeed cultural) history of mankind is entering a seriously new phase; so that if we want to understand it we must study it, and not study something else: namely, traditional religion.

Is the current development of man's religiousness being worked out inside the mosques? in the temples? in the churches?

I somewhat doubt it; or at least, I suspect not only there. I would advise, let us say a Japanese scholar who might wish to study the present-day evolution of *homo religiosus* in American, not to confine his investigations totally to the formally institutionalized Church, even though Christians especially in recent centuries have formally institutionalized their religious life more than perhaps is true of any other society on earth, either at present or throughout the past. Yet one obvious development on this continent, worth his keeping an eye on, is the emergence of religion departments in arts faculties, and the possibility that intellectual creativity may be shifting from the seminaries to them, the possibility that it may be there that alone will be answered the questions that even the Church itself is asking. Yet this, I say, is a fairly obvious point; there are many much more covert and subtle. Similarly, I would advise any Western scholar who sets out to study modern religious process in the Islamic world, not to imagine that he either knows or can find out what Islam formally or essentially is before he starts, so that his task is to survey the current scene and simply to report on what is happening to *that* Islam in the tumult of today's whirlwind. Similarly for something that he conceives as "Hinduism," some traditional form.

The Islam that is significant today lies as it always has lain, in the heart of Muslims, and not necessarily in the inherited forms. The "Hinduism" that it is our task to describe is that spirit astir among Hindus whose formulation lies in the future, not in the past. Our concern today is with those things that will become traditions tomorrow, or the day after; quite possibly, long after we are dead. Traditions now extant are the deposit of earlier men's faith. At best, they can be the efficient cause of the faith of man today. Yet if there is one quality characteristic of our modern age, it is the possibility of dislocation between faith and inherited formulation. An investigation concerned only with formulation, not with faith, will all too probably miss the heart of the matter.

Illustrative of this kind of point is Dag Hammarskjöld's *Markings*. Until this book appeared, a formalistic student of contemporary religious life in the West would hardly have known that this gentleman represented an important part of what he ought to be studying. Suppose that the United Nations Secretary-General had had the kind of concern and vision and question that apparently he did have, yet had not written these memoirs or, he having written them, they had not been published. Does any one of us seriously imagine that there are no counterparts to Hammarskjöld in the modern Muslim or Hindu or Buddhist or African worlds, whose reflections have not and never will appear in published form?

Even this, however, only hints at the fundamental point that I wish to make. For even Hammarskjöld, although his life was manifestly of the sort that is designated by "modern culture," and its religious quality was manifestly *not* of the sort designated by "traditional religion," yet to express this quality nonetheless used in the intimacy of his private meditation language that is continuous with certain strands in the overt religious tradition of his society, particularly those of the mystics. I have Muslim and a few Hindu friends who do the same, though outwardly their lives are what any anthropologist would call secular. Beyond even this group, however, is another realm perhaps no less important but still more subtle and elusive: the religiousness of men who either do not express their religiousness formally at all, or if they do, express it in new, untraditional, ways.

If not fully or necessarily in what is called tradition, then, where is the religious life of modern man to be found? Let me discuss this question in two stages.

First, using the concepts "tradition" and "faith" that in *The Meaning and End of Religion* I have proposed as applicable respectively to the external and the internal aspects of man's religious life, we may say that a person's faith is the meaning that his tradition has for him, if it is religiously meaningful. Yet we must quickly go on to say, because of the comprehensive nature of religious response, that a person's faith is the meaning that life has for him, in the light of his tradition. Modern secularist society postulates a "religious factor" as one element in the pattern of life, alongside other factors such as the economic, the political, the legal, and in such cases as our title, also the cultural. The modern West, further, tried for a time to impose such an analysis on other societies and the lives of other men. Yet this, we are discovering, is to misunderstand. Faith is not a factor in a man's life, alongside others. It may be engendered and nurtured primarily (though never exclusively) by one factor in the social complex. Yet once it has arisen in personal life (which is the only place that it can arise), if it is authentic, it embraces, and colours, all. It is not one element in the total pattern of that person's life; rather, it *is* the pattern that the other elements form.

To understand a man's faith is to ascertain how he sees the world (and feels it)—all of the world, from economics to art, from failure in an examination to the crying of a neighbour's child. If a man loses his faith, it may be that no one of the factors in his life has changed; the difference is simply that they no longer cohere into an integrated pattern. A Muslim's faith is not one more item in a list of the things that make up his life; it is the meaning that the other items have. When they cease to have meaning, his faith is gone.

"Traditional religion," to use that Western term, as one item in his own or his society's life, may indeed have become one of those factors that surround him but do not have much transcendent meaning for him; it may no longer serve him as a catalyst enabling him to find significance in life, and indeed in death. When this happens, it has become interesting to the historian of culture, but is no longer really the subject-matter of the historian of religion.

In other words, the subject-matter of our study, if we are to do justice to what we have taken on, is not merely tradition but faith; not merely the overt manifestations of man's religious life, but that life itself. The distinction is always important, but especially so in cases where these manifestations are no longer playing, or are perhaps no longer playing, a vital and self-transcending role. In the study of religion one's concern is not primarily the doctrines and scriptures and prayers and rites and institutions but, rather, what these do to a man. Not the tribal dance, so much as what happens to the African dancing; not the caste system, so much as what kind of person the Hindu becomes within it, or without it; not the *mudra* of the statuary so much as how a Buddhist is changed by contemplating it; not the Qur'an so much as what the Qur'an means to a Muslim.

While this is true in general, it leads on to my second stage, which is the pith of my answer to our particular question about religiousness in modern times. If it be recognized, as I think it must, that the interesting thing about outward religious phenomena in the past is that they expressed and nourished an inner orientation in the personal lives of those for whom they were religiously meaningful, then it follows that the significant question for us as students and scholars today is not primarily: What is happening in modern times to those traditions? Rather, the central question that we are called upon to treat is the momentous one: What is happening in our day to the qualities of life that those traditions used to represent and to foster? Religious life has always been a matter of symbols. The history of man's religious life today is the story not merely, and perhaps not even primarily, of those inherited symbols, but rather, of what is afoot among men in regard to what has been symbolized.

What has been happening in our century among Indian Muslims, and what is happening today in Pakistan, to the courage and serenity that the Islamic system traditionally inspired in its adherents? To the sense of order, and the aspiration to justice, that the *shari'ah* traditionally signified? To the integrity that the traditional Islamic education inspired, the forbearance, the confidence, the intellectual acumen, the humility?

The religious history of the Hindu community is a history in part, no doubt, of traditional ceremonial and ideological and sociological pattern. Yet in more significant part it is a history, however difficult this may be to discern, of fortitude and of quiet humaneness, of a conviction that life is worth living, and death worth dying, that goals are worth striving for, that the immediate is caught up in the eternal. The Buddhist metaphors served to kindle in the mind and heart of the Buddhist the perhaps unconscious awareness that one's own fortune is not a reason for gloating, or one's neighbour's fortune, for envy; that knowledge is more important than wealth, and wisdom than knowledge; that the world is to be appreciated, and not merely exploited; that one's fellow is to be treated as an end, not merely as a means; that sorrow is not a reason for despair.

To what extent, and in what ways, are those same metaphors kindling such an awareness today? That is our problem. If "traditional religion" is not kindling it, what is? If it is not being kindled, what is happening to the man, and to the society, that used to have it? Or is some new awareness dawning, some new vision?

I do not wish to suggest that in the past, life was all virtue or all transcendence; or that in the present it is all bleakness or vacuity. All that I contend is that in the past, insofar as there *was* virtue or transcendence, insofar as the life of man was distinguished from that of the brutes, to that extent religiousness was at play. This is what religiousness is all about; and the particular forms that we call Hinduism and the rest are simply the forms in which these men expressed these facts. And I am contending that in the present, insofar as man's spirit is still alive and creative, then our business is to try to discern where its liveliness and creativity are, how they are nourished, and how they are expressed; insofar as man's life is still meaningful, what its meaning is, and how this meaningfulness is induced and communicated.

We have not discharged our task simply by tracing the current fate of past expressions of man's spiritual life. Our adventure is much more demanding: to discover and to report how far and wherein those inherited symbols are today performing their earlier function as one part of one side of the complex dialectic between man's spirit and his material environment; and insofar as they are performing it only partially or haltingly or are perhaps no longer performing it, then how far and wherein that spirit is starved or stifled or momentarily suppressed or latent, and also how far and wherein it has found or is finding or is searching for new symbols; and how far and wherein the spirit of man in various particular parts of the globe is in fact doing what some observers despondently or triumphantly suggest: namely, learning to live without symbols, expressing its hopes and fears and aspirations and resolutions and its vision and courage and love directly, replacing poetry with prose.

Man's capacity to feel at home in the universe; to find humility in himself even at his most triumphant, and cosmic significance in himself even at his most wretched, and in his neighbour even at *his* most wretched; to choose, and to know that his choice is right or wrong, and that it matters; to respond, and to know oneself responded to— where are these today? And how?

It is easier to answer these questions for an Indian village than it is for Bombay or Dacca; easier to answer them for an Iqbal or a Krishnaswami than for an Ayyub or a C. V. Raman; easier to answer them for a new marriage law than for a new tax law. Yet easy or hard, to answer them is our assignment, our challenge.

I close this essay with a specifically professional point. Some will perhaps wish to comment that this realm of inquiry is too delicate, or too grand, that methodologically the academic scholar is equipped to handle only more prosaic, more "objective" questions. Some of us, however, reject the new scholasticism that would give priority to discipline over subject-matter, and would exclude from consideration all facets of a problem that do not neatly fit one's extant techniques. In the study of human affairs such a curtailed approach is not merely inadequate but falsifying: we can limit the circumference of our inquiry but not the depth of our concern, and if our methods prove not adequate to the dimensions of what we are studying then we must find or construct new methods.

And this, in fact, I would suggest, is what is discernibly happening. A new venture in religious scholarship is coming into being, perhaps especially on the North American continent, but it will have no substance until it is collaborative across the world.

It is a venture whose aspirations are indeed grand and transcend those that have previously been standard, even though its accomplishments are as yet incipient and its methods groping. For all its uncertainties, something novel is afoot, and in my judgment something powerful.

The new study will include, for instance, phenomenology of

religion but will pass well beyond it. For one thing, one thinks of the philosophic divergence, even in Europe, between phenomenologists and existentialists; of the two, one could argue that the latter are perhaps no less close to the religionist's orientation. This is perhaps at least as significant as the more standardly recognized divergence between phenomenologists and historians, which we are already overcoming. Besides these, may I speculate that perhaps one of the reasons for the new expansion in our studies may have to do with an awareness of the point on which I have touched, that the religiousness of contemporary man may conceivably be, at least in part, without phenomena (as Hammarskjöld's almost was). Dietrich Bonhoeffer's "religionless Christianity" is perhaps a straw in what one might perhaps call the possibility of a wind of phenomenon-less religion—or better, a religionless faith.

Indeed, it was Brede Kristensen himself who said that our final concern is less with the phenomena than with what these mean to men for whom they are avenues of faith. One might lay it down virtually as a rule that, as the phenomenologists of religion themselves have recognized, man's religiousness always transcends phenomena; and I have argued that what has been called the study of religion must be recognized, rather, as the study not primarily of things but of persons. This, I would contend, is always true; and most of all for the study of today, when even such pehnomena as there are may be different from the traditionalist ones. I suppose that my entire thesis can be summed up in the affirmation that the study of religion must be fundamentally a study of persons. Comparative religion is the study of man in his religious diversity. Through it, man is striving to become conscious of himself in his fragmented relation to transcendence.

NOTES

1. "Final Circular Letter" for the eleventh congress of the International Association for the History of Religions, dated November, 1964.

2. "Second Circular Letter," dated June, 1964.

5

The Meaning of Modernization*

Unlike the first four selections, this essay is not explicitly about religion and was not addressed to an audience concerned with the promotion or with the description of religion. Yet it contributes to this anthology in more ways than one.

First, it supplements the essay on "Traditional Religions and Modern Culture" by providing the explicit discussion of modernity which was lacking there. Just as, in Smith's thought, "religions" are not static entities, it turns out that modernity is not a static entity either. It is not a particular institution that a population can have or enjoy; in a somewhat extended discussion Smith establishes the point that different things can constitute modernity for different people. Modernity, rather, is a quality of acting and choosing, a quality of self-conscious control and direction of one's own destiny. In some respects therefore it resembles Smith's conception of "faith" as an outlook implicit in living rather than as an entity to be possessed.

Second, this essay was first delivered as an address not to a Western but to an Asian audience. It was the opening lecture in a set of three by Smith on "Modernisation of a Traditional Society," delivered in New Delhi as the annual lecture series of the

* Reprinted in slightly abridged form from Wilfred Cantwell Smith, *Modernisation of a Traditional Society* (Bombay: Asia Publishing House, 1965), pp. 1–22. Copyright by Wilfred Cantwell Smith. Used by permission.

*Indian Council of World Affairs on March 23–25, 1964. Smith
was, then, talking with Indians, at their invitation, about the
present-day practical and moral concerns of their own country,
this selection being the more theoretical preamble to his remarks.
Since the eighth selection in this anthology will present the view
that an acceptable description of a people's tradition must be
acceptable to the people being described, the inclusion of an
explicit conversation of Smith with Indian (in this case, chiefly
Hindu) intellectuals may prove illustrative.*

*A third point, which this selection may contribute in passing,
is Smith's own allusion in retrospect to what some of his social
ideals had been during his first years in India, two decades earlier. His first book, written in those years,* Modern Islam in
India: A Social Analysis, *had more affinities with Marxist
thought than does his subsequent work. Although Smith manifestly retains a fundamental view of history as process, the nature
of his disillusionment with the course that Marxist régimes took
is touched upon here.*

*If Smith were to speak to an American audience today on the
topic of modernization, his remarks would be different. Particularly this essay's optimism concerning historical development and
the possibilities for conscious choice might need to be toned
down. He indicates, in correspondence: "I had not yet moved to
the United States."*—ED.

Historians of ideas know well enough that a notion of "progress"
was dominant in the nineteenth century in the West. One secondary concept from the idea of progress lurks still not only in
the minds of men-in-the-street but in the minds, and therefore in
the activities, of quite important, responsible, persons. This is the
concept "modern." It seems an innocent idea, straightforward
and simple, though on scrutiny it turns out to be less innocent
than one had thought. If things are getting better all the time,
steadily, relentlessly, then it follows that to be modern is good;
the very term "modern" then means "something valuable,"

something nearer to one's heart's desire. Once one is no longer persuaded, however, that progress is inherent and self-generating, once one begins to wonder whether human folly or wickedness, apathy or inadvertence, may divert or frustrate and even perhaps reverse whatever trends toward perfection may be at work in the world, then the meaning of "modern," if not shattered, must at least become less clear. The conviction, or assumption, that the term "modern" designates something desirable stands or falls, I submit, with the belief that progress in human affairs can be relied upon as inevitable.

Indeed, may we not also assert that something of this sort applies even to the very supposition that the term means anything at all? If the world is moving ineluctably, incontrovertibly, towards some goal that is both fixed and known, however vaguely, towards some tomorrow that is somehow guaranteed, then "modern" means closer to that goal, more like it. If, on the other hand, the future is not given, definite and unchangeable, or even if it is given but not known, then what does "modern" mean? If we do not know the destiny of human life on earth, how are we to tell whether something is modern or not, except in the rather useless sense that everything that exists today is modern? If "modern" means "in line with the basic trend of events," but if we do not know what the trend of events is, where it is leading, what becomes of our word? To phrase the matter in another fashion, one might suggest that to ask, "What does modernization mean?" is in effect to ask, "Where are we going?"

You may possibly agree that this latter question is becoming less easy to answer as we go along. I lived in India first for six years in the 1940's, before Partition and Independence. In those days I was younger, of course, more naïve and enthusiastic and with more buoyant optimism; but the situation itself seemed simpler. The zest of the nationalist movement carried us all along, with a program that was simple at least in the sense of being straightforward: "Let's remove British rule and get to work." Some of us, in addition, were socialists, in the simple days

before the devastation of the Stalin terror had become revealed,
before imperialist aggression in Hungary and China. Those were
messianic days, with the brave new world just round the corner.
The task facing humanity might not be easy, yet it was simple.
Perhaps it was only negative: if we just got rid of the British, or
of the bourgeoisie, or of communalism [the allegiance to ethnic
or religious group membership in Indian life], all would be well.
We might have to work hard to attain the goal, but the goal
itself seemed to be given: it existed in the future, if not in the
then present; as an ideal, if not yet as an actuality. And the
reality, the truth of the ideal, seemed independent of ourselves:
we had to strive to attain it, and even perhaps to recognize it, but
not to concoct it. Our job was to realize it on earth, but not to
construct it in heaven.

Now that the immediate goals of our youth have been
achieved—national independence in India, the liquidation of
Western imperialism, the welfare state in Britain, the achievement of the proletarian revolution in half of Asia—we find that
men's responsibilities for running the world bring vagueness in
our sense of what actually we now want, as well as perplexity as
to what actually we are getting. We used to be more confident
that we knew what tomorrow would look like.

The possibility that things may go wrong—a possibility more
vividly in our minds today perhaps both in India and in Western
society—means that modernity may be less charming, and is
anyway less clear, than we used to suppose. At least, I am proposing that it will repay inquiry to ask what we really do mean
when we say "modern," and what we ought to mean.

First, we may observe readily enough that the term "modern"
is presumed to mean something good; there exists much enthusi-
asm for the notion of modernizing. But that "modern" necessarily means "desirable" will not stand up to a moment's reflection. Nothing is more modern, I suppose, than nuclear weapons,
or the horrendous possibility that the human race can in a flash
commit global suicide or at least level civilizations to the ground.
Bacteriological warfare is so unthinkable in its loathsomeness

that we simply do not think about it, even though it is perhaps more awful than the atomic menace; yet it is superbly a modern threat. Again, if democracy is modern in the world, even more modern is fascism. The efficiency of its wickedness, and the scale of its oppression, are historically unprecedented. Or if these be dismissed somehow as aberrations (itself an interesting concept) or anyway as un-Indian examples, let us turn to more specifically Indian contexts.

One example relevant to India is the industrial slum, a facet of the sprawling urbanization process that marks, for instance, the characteristically *modern* cities of Bombay and Calcutta. Industrial urban slums, the historian notes, are a relatively modern development. An even clearer instance is population increase. Both the absolute numbers of people in India today, and the frightening rate at which those massive numbers are increasing and will, we are told, increasingly increase—these are modern. Not only are they recent in the straightforward sense of being historically unprecedented, but also they are modern in that they rest squarely on the whole substance and apparatus of modernity in the world: on medicine and scientific hygiene, on technological communications systems and efficient social institutions, on welfare-state structures and ideas. The population explosion and its threat are peculiarly modern affairs.

In fact, in *many* ways modernity is a threat. For many thousands of years geography protected India: in many directions from foreign conquest, and in all cases from foreign rule. In ancient times anyone who dominated India, however alien, had to settle down in the land and therefore to become in some degree Indian. It was with the beginning of a modern process that the country could be conquered from the sea and ruled from the outside by foreigners who remained foreigners. Still more modern is the failure of the northeastern geographic barrier to afford protection. For centuries upon centuries China could never threaten India across the lofty Himalayas. It is a *modern* fact, in every sense of the word, that India should face danger from that unexpected quarter.

As external aggression is possible in new forms, so also is internal subversion: the novel capacity of a ruthless power, if one such were to seize control in India, not only to replace the central government but to reach out into previously inaccessible villages, and by modern totalitarian methods to break the continuity of popular culture, even to smash a religious heritage.

There are modern problems, not merely modern amenities.

Once the point is pressed, of course, no one will actually defend the idea that everything new, without exception, is admirable; that every single change, actual or potential, is a change for the better. We can all think of innovations that are not welcome. Even the enthusiasts for modernization do not really intend a blanket approval of everything that happens. In fact, may we not conclude that for those who applaud the "modern" there is a crucial though unnoticed difference in meaning between "modern" and "recent" or "new"?

One of the prominent elder statesmen of the Ataturk régime in Turkey, a grand and able leader, told me once when I was visiting him in his ancestral home in Istanbul that certain repairs that were being made in the house had needed doing again although they had been attended to only two years previously, whereas the same repairs, effected when he was a boy, had lasted forty-four years. In other words, the workmanship of the artisans at the turn of the century had been of such a quality as to last almost a lifetime, whereas their successors in recent times did the same job in such a slipshod and insouciant way that the work needed re-doing after only two years. Now he would not have reported this to me, in a long and serious discussion on the Turkish revolution, had he not regarded it, and presented it, as typical of a trend (which we were discussing) towards a less responsible and less fastidious attitude on the part of craftsmen towards their tasks, in modern times. I would not have appreciated his illustration nor remembered it, had I not been vividly familiar with just the same sort of development in Canada.

Such a trend in Turkey, in Canada, and no doubt in India and in other lands, is presumably a world-wide emergence of the depersonalization of labour, the tendency to work for monetary gain rather than out of a joy and pride in craftsmanship, the loss of a fusion of a sense of moral responsibility and ultimate personal significance with the mundane task at hand. If such a process is occurring throughout the world, so that everywhere workers are finding it less and less normal to derive integrity and satisfaction from a job well done, shall we label it "modern"? When we talk of modernizing India quickly, do we in part mean an attempt to accelerate this particular development? It may be new; but is it what we intend by "modern"?

From our first main point, that not everything new is good, we move to our second point: that not everything contemporary is modern.

We all mean by "modern" something else than mere date. But what? Motor cars are more modern than bullock carts, I suppose everyone will affirm. The scooter rickshaw in India is a newer phenomenon in urban public transportation than is the taxi, though some people, if they can afford it, still prefer the old-fashioned taxi. Do bullock carts, Cadillacs, scooters constitute a series in that order? The fact that scooters, "mopeds" [pedal bicycles fitted with a small motor], and the like are in some ways more relevant to the economic and climatic and democratic conditions of India than are Cadillacs, makes this question a serious one. An answer is not immediately evident. If standards of chemistry teaching in schools are going down, or of English, or of self-discipline, is this then modern? Should the modernizer support every tendency that the statistician discerns?

One may consider the case of the traditionalist for whom what is good lies in the past, in some classical or golden age of long ago, or even just the way things were when he was growing up, and who decries contemporary life as an aberration or betrayal. If he be a revivalist, an active conservative, then his program is to reintroduce what has once been, to re-implement his traditionalist ideal. And if he succeeds tomorrow, then will not what is current today be superseded by what, then, is truly modern, or soon will be: namely, that re-actualized ideal? If *that* is what tomorrow is going to look like, then are those of us who have a different aspiration or vision simply wrong, including being wrong in our sense of what the word "modern" rightly means? For example, those who would revive Sanskrit must hold that to learn Sanskrit is the modern thing to do, and that for an Indian to know only English and Hindi and Tamil or to be content with them is old-fashioned—or soon will be.

The very fact that one can speak of modernizing India is itself interesting. Apparently the idea is that the land can become, and should be made, more modern than it now is, even though everything that exists in India today exists, after all, in the present moment. In a purely empirical sense, the status quo in India is a modern fact. Indeed, a Westerner who knows and appreciates contemporary India as it stands is a more modern person, I might urge, than is his uneducated neighbour who knows only his local Western environment—even if that be replete with up-to-date plumbing and all the gadgets.

Or if a society can be made more modern, should one think of "modernizing" the United States? Am I right in thinking that most people feel, without analysing the idea much, that the United States not only is already modern but also is becoming more modern day by day (I personally would question both these, in part), whereas in the case of India they feel that the land may be modernized, may be *made* more modern than it is, but only through effort, only if one works at it? In this view, there would seem to be a process of modernization which is automatically and inexorably taking place in some parts of the world, while in other parts, such as India, it might not take place and indeed will not unless men exert themselves and push it.

If some parts of the United States are more modern than others —as I suppose would have to be conceded by those who regard the United States in general as somehow more modern than, say, Thailand—then what precisely is the relation of those persons or areas there that are more modern, to the modernizing process? Is prosperity normal, and poverty an aberration? Is technological progress standard, even if not ubiquitous, so that one fails to get

it in certain regions where particular obstacles to it have somehow come into play but otherwise it just takes place? Or are the
"backward" parts of the United States just as normal as the
"modern" ones, only by a different norm? The terms "backward"
and "advanced" imply that the parts that we do not like are
static, or are moving slowly, while what we approve is dynamic—
suggesting again that the direction is given, even though the
speed is not. I doubt that we really believe this, however. Can
things not move in various directions, as well as at various
speeds?

Can the United States and the Soviet Union both be modern
but in different ways? Or insofar as they both become truly
modern, will they to that extent necessarily converge? We cannot
be sure that modernity will have to be uniform. Could India
become modern in quite a different way yet—a third or second
modernity? How radically different can various meanings for our
term be? If a modernized India will look different from modernized Germany, then the question of what "modern" signifies becomes still more difficult.

The relation of "modernization" to "Westernization" can bear
closer scrutiny. Probably the person who has the least trouble of
all with the term "modern" for things in India is the casual
Western tourist, the more naïve the better. The less a visitor
knows of India, the less he appreciates its complexities and its
history, the less sensitive he is to its culture, then the more readily and glibly does he talk of the contrast between "ancient" and
"modern." Their stark juxtaposition elicits his most pointed
comments, and he is least troubled by any doubt as to which is
which. If he sees something with which he is familiar at home,
and which he likes—whether hotdog or university, large plate-
glass windows or night-club cabaret—he calls it "modern,"
whereas things that are characteristically Indian and new to him,
especially if he does not understand them or like them, he calls
exotic, traditional, or ancient. In the West, ice cream is a fairly
recent innovation, whereas the institution of monogamous marriage is an ancient heritage, and horse racing is intermediate,

some centuries old; yet he does not think it incongruous to find
the family of an American jockey enjoying ice cream. An equally
mixed situation in India, however, he might well label a stark
"contrast."

Something of this sort applies even to certain more sophisticated observers and even various "experts." I have known political scientists to use quite seriously the categories "traditional
state" and "modern state" in their study of the Near East, for
instance; as though these two types exhausted the possibilities,
their criterion of "modern" being the closeness to the state-form
of the West. Yet one may ask whether the traditional Western
state is really modern. Once it was, perhaps, but is it so any
more? An hypothesis could conceivably be propounded that the
territorial nation-state, secular, domestically neutralist, is a basically nineteenth-century phenomenon, while the newer twentieth-
century emergence is, rather, the ideological state—citing the
Soviet Union and China, Israel and Pakistan as instances. One
may not approve of ideological states, but then there are doubtless many trends in the modern world of which one does not
approve. Or, contrariwise, one might approve warmly, contending that many of the new states of Africa and Asia will flounder
until they can find for themselves, instead of the alien and imitative Western basis, some ideological *raison d'être* and dynamic
attuned to the culture and aspirations of their own populace.
Whether one approves or not is distinct from the question of
whether this development is in fact taking place.

And whether it is in fact taking place is perhaps distinct from
a question of whether or not it is "modern." Does the modernization of India signify that the country should abandon its secularist democratic aspiration, and substitute some dogmatic totali-
tarianism, Hindu or whatever? Some would answer this with a
"no" and would continue to answer it with a "no" regardless of
what course other new nations might adopt in South Asia or
further afield. In other words, these men would be contending
that the meaning of "modernization" for India is to be determined not by what happens outside India.

While the question of how India's modernization is to be determined internally remains unanswered, it is clear that the matter is not to be defined in terms of the West's evolution. Yet how widespread the facile fallacy seems to be that "modernization" and "Westernization" are interchangeable terms. If such a thesis were held deliberately, the arguments could be analysed, but it is a glib and unconscious error, an unexamined confusion.

To return to the foreign tourist—and, alas, sometimes also the foreign "expert": I have sometimes thought that one might entitle a short essay concerning such outsiders "On Seeing What Is Not There." A Westerner coming to India for the first time is quite likely to be struck most forcibly by those things that he does *not* find. He has grown up accustomed to taking several things for granted, and when he discovers that they are missing, he is excited by their absence—so much so that he may give virtually his whole attention to what is not there, to the point of hardly seeing or caring what is. In fact, it requires a rather unusual temperament or orientation, or else quite a long time, or both, to become truly aware of what actually is the Indian situation: what is going on, what it is that needs to be modernized. Almost the whole problem for anyone coming from the outside as a student is to learn, slowly, patiently, to see India as it is.

There are well-meaning outsiders in administrative and operational positions whose notion of modernizing any African or Asian country is uncritically and simply to introduce Western patterns (the only ones they know). It is not that they have thought through the situation, assessed the historical dynamics and social potentialities of the people they have come to aid, and have concluded that in this quite special situation the most effective means to modernize is to adopt a Western model. No; they assume without reflection that "modern" *means* Western. I have often wondered whether every foreign adviser sent to any African or Asian country should not be required to spend his first year passively learning, before he sets out on any active program of assistance. It would slow things down in the short run, but perhaps over the long run it might prove expeditious.

There are, I think, three major reasons why India, to the extent that it wants to, or any non-Western community, cannot just copy the West in its transformations, and cannot even find the meaning or content of modernization by simply inquiring from the West.

Of my three reasons, the first is the obvious one—that India is different. At a profound level, metaphysical and moral, I am a humanist with massive conviction that man as man, wherever he may be found, in whatever condition, in whatever context, is one. In part, I derive this faith from my Christian religious tradition; in part, I spend my time carrying on a campaign with other representatives of my tradition trying to persuade them to take this matter more seriously, more rigorously, more radically than has ever been done. I totally and committedly believe that the whole of mankind essentially does, and practically must, form one community. Only, I imagine that it will be a multiform, not a uniform, community at least for the proximate future. So far as India is concerned, then, I am not one of those who hold that the country cannot manage democracy or secularism or technology, or cannot hope for prosperity and abundance. All I am contending is that, starting from a different basis, it will most profitably take somewhat different paths to arrive at similar goals, or contrariwise, that the same procedures may lead to differing results.

(My study of a non-Western civilization—the Islamic—over the past twenty or thirty years has persuaded me that, both in its relation to the West and in its relation to Hindu culture, the ultimate unity and the proximate differences of differing communities are much more profound than superficial observation would suggest—much more ramifying operationally, much more significant practically.)

Let me illustrate my thesis that India's differences from the West must exact differences in modernization. One difference, striking to a Canadian, is climate; almost any technique or structure suited to Western Europe or North America may have to be modified for India because of the differences in climate. This is not a question of better or worse. To take a more important illustration, consider religion. Western secularism involves a separation of State and Church, whereas neither the Hindu nor the Muslim community possesses an organized religious incorporation of the church type [and "secularism" in India implies not dominantly a non-religious personal view of the world but, rather, what can be termed pluralism, the equal status of religious communities as groups in the state—ED.]. Law stands in quite a different relation to the Muslim's orientation, again differently to the Hindu's, from that to the Christian's. And so on. Thus in many ways it is meaningless to speak of religion's playing the same role in Western society and in Indian.

Or, if these two examples, material and spiritual, seem *recherchés*, let us consider the language question, of Indian vernaculars *versus* English. In my judgment, no one has begun to appreciate the life of India who has not felt the force of the argument against the retention of English as the medium in its universities, felt it agonizingly to the point of recognizing it as virtually unanswerable; while at the same time, anyone who has failed to recognize the almost unanswerable force of the argument against *abandoning* English is also, surely, insensitive and unaware. The weight, delicacy, and intractability of this issue in Indian intellectual life are formidable. Yet it is a question that in this form the West does not face, does not appreciate, and on which its example is not of consequence. It is surely foolish to imagine that India can become modern without solving this central problem. Yet it is one that it must solve itself, there being no Western solution to import, whether good or bad. The West, then, is different from India; potentially helpful as some sort of guide, but inadequate as a model.

Secondly, the question of modernization in India cannot be given a simple Western answer because there is no simple Western answer. The West, too, is groping. The West, too, is in process, is in the swift-flowing stream of change; so that it too, after a period of relative confidence as to direction, is itself now uncertain on that score.

For a time, the leaders of Western culture had considerable

assurance that the goal was more or less agreed (or at least could become so), so that intelligence and effort could be spent chiefly on ways and means of attaining it. The meaning of "modernization," to use our own terms, was thought to be more or less known (or at least knowable). Today, however, when on the one hand certain immediate goals have already been achieved, and on the other hand new possibilities, for both good and evil, far beyond what was pondered until recently, are being opened up for further development, leaders in the West are increasingly aware that the future is not given, that the directions are not fixed, that the responsibility for effective choosing is theirs, or at least is society's. They are recognizing that the future will be largely what man makes it; so that the task of human history is not merely to strive towards a goal, but to choose, to discern, or even to construct, a goal.

The meaning of the modernization process is no longer given by the direction in which the West is moving. For Western development is becoming increasingly self-conscious, exploratory, existential—so that that development will increasingly explicate, rather than determine, ideas as to human destiny. Modernity is no longer a goal but a process; no longer something to adopt, but something to participate in. It is not something that one has, but something that one does, and does well or badly. We in the West, we realize, may do it badly; and perhaps others may also.

My third reason, however, for affirming that modernization for India cannot copy the West, follows at once. For, if the most important present-day emergence in Western history is an enlarged self-consciousness, perhaps also the most important single new ingredient in that consciousness is its new global quality. It transcends the West, to embrace, at least ideally, all mankind. To put the point in an aphorism, the fully modern West is no longer Western; no longer, that is, exclusively Western, within the boundaries of its own civilization. A Westerner who is still essentially Western is not quite modern, is too provincial to be modern. The categories "Western" and "Oriental," or more accurately, "Western," "Islamic," "Indian," "East Asian," etc., have been exceedingly important—it is my professional business to say how important. Yet they are today in the process of being superseded, however incipiently, by a new cosmopolitanism. By this I do not mean simply that Western minds are beginning to take all the world as their purview; an Asian audience would quickly detect and resent the arrogance in that. What I mean, rather, is that alert minds in the West are asking no longer, "Where is the West going?" but rather, "Where is the world going?" And they are aware that they cannot themselves answer such a question, but that it must and will be answered in colloquy by Western, Islamic, Indian, African, and Communist minds (and hearts) together.

The modernization of the West cannot be defined in terms of the West's future, for the West does not have a future of its own. It can look forward intelligently only to the Western strand in the future of the world—a future that all of us must and will construct jointly, for good or ill.

Even our ideal of the future, even if we fail to achieve it, must be an ideal of one world, which means in effect an ideal that all of us can jointly approve. I am arguing that no intelligent Westerner can today posit for himself or for his society an objective or target other than one to which an Asian or African can subscribe. For only so can it be global; and, therefore, only so can it be either realistic or desirable. This means, a target that they and he shall have jointly elaborated. In other words, what Westerners shall mean from now on by modernization as a conscious process, is a question that they cannot answer for India because they cannot answer it even for themselves without India's participation. A continuingly modernizing West involves its increasing integration in the total modern world, in which an increasingly modernizing India must be an increasingly constituent part.

This is as much true in economics and in religion as it is in meteorology or linguistics. The modernization of the rest of the world (of America, of Russia, of Pakistan, or Israel and the rest) waits in part on an answer to that question in India, and vice versa. The modernization of India and the continuing modernization of the West are both questions that are giving way to a larger, more complex, more searching question as to the modernization of a world that includes both India and the West, includes China and Africa and the rest. To think of modernizing India only in Indian terms, or only in Western terms, or even in Indian *and* Western terms, whatever else it may be, is not modern.

Wealth is not something that a society has, but something that it does. Even those who think of a modernized India as a richly productive India are still involved in the question of how to arrive at that happy condition and the question of what such an India will look like. The word "modern" may mean "economically productive," but it cannot mean *only* that. For, a society that produces and consumes a lot of goods is different from a society of privation—different not only economically, but socially, intellectually, medically, politically, educationally, artistically, and, I will argue, even morally and religiously. Whether the other various differences precede or follow the economic difference, is worth asking. The modernizing process is not defined or clarified, at least not finally, by simply opining that abundance should displace scarcity. Part of the fundamental problem in all this realm is the glib tendency of many to think of modernism as almost a commodity, something that can be imported or added on, something that can be bought and paid for; so that once you have it you can then relax and enjoy it passively. This idea is not only wrong, but dangerous. Modernism, I repeat, is not to adopt but to participate in; not to have, but to do and to be. And not even to be, but to keep becoming—a process, an orientation, a dynamic.

To sum up. I have argued that not everything modern is good; indeed, some of modernity is horrifying. Not everything recent is modern; indeed, some is retrogressive. To modernize is not the same as to Westernize; for how is the West to pursue, or to betray, it? Modernization is something that we seem to want desperately, but we have not yet been able to say what it is.

My suggestion is that although an intelligent man cannot accept any of the popular connotations as they stand, yet he can learn from each, and the answer that he will formulate for himself will preserve significant ingredients from each of the popular misconceptions, avoiding the pitfalls. Can we define our term in such a way that modernization remains good, yet recognizes potential disaster; that it remains new, yet is discriminating; that it remains applicable to the West, yet not to all of the West, and applies to India in particular, yet universally; that it means something precise, yet does not define the future so as to cancel out freedom? These are minimum tests. I suggest that they can, in fact, be met.

I said at the beginning that the concept "modern" involves a sense that history is moving in a particular direction; and this still seems to be the crux of our problem. For we do not really know where history is moving. Indeed—and this is decisive—our very modernity enables us to make it move either this way or that. Uncertainty is not a failure of our being modern, but a consequence of it. Man cannot tell how men will use the vast new powers that modernity has provided. We do not and cannot know how history in general will unfold. Yet in one area, we can assert a linear development, in one unmistakable, irreversible direction: namely, the progress of science, with its offspring technology, and the accumulation of knowledge generally. Who can say whether or not there is "progress" in art, in morals, in saintliness, in wisdom, in family life? Is ours the *kali yug* [the degenerate age], and was there really a golden age of yore—or will there be one soon? In all other realms opinions differ in their assessment of the past; and even those who argue for progress admit that it cannot be guaranteed for the future. Tomorrow man may misuse his opportunities. In the one realm of accumulating knowledge, however—both on the technical side, in experimental science; and in general, in human awareness of time and space, history and geography, and man's understanding of his own behaviour—a steady and indeed brilliant, spectacular, march forward has become evident, and seems likely to continue. How we shall use our knowledge and our science, no one knows;

but about our knowledge and our science it is safe to affirm that they have grown and are growing.

Applied, this ever greater knowledge has been transforming human life by making available to us a vast and ever increasing new range of possibilities, increasing our power to act and the sweep of our choice, and increasing our awareness. There is nothing to tell us *how* we shall be using this new power, nothing to establish which of the many new choices open to us we shall in fact choose, nothing to predetermine how we shall behave in the light of our new self-consciousness, our new awareness of ourselves and of nature, of history and of our global, universal context. But it is the power itself, the fact of choosing, the awareness of context, that are modern—and that, nothing, once we have them, can take away. There is nothing essentially modern in choosing any particular one of A or B or C or D . . . or P or Q . . . or Y or Z; what is modern is our ability to choose among so many, where our ancestors had no alternative to A, or at most choice only between A and B. We may even choose A, as they did. So long as we do so deliberately, self-consciously, responsibly, knowing that it is a fateful choice over against all the others, then it is still modern—just as it is modern to choose Q or Z, of which those ancestors never dreamed.

Science has provided the machines that can move mountains, divert rivers, turn deserts into gardens—or gardens into deserts. Knowledge and techniques today enable governments to transform societies, change language, increase or curtail freedom, advance or ruin health. Persuaders can entice men to drink Coca-Cola or to stop smoking, to riot over inflamed passions or to be discontent with only one family car. Men have the knowledge and the power to shape the environment in which they shall live.

To be modern does not mean to live in one particular kind of environment rather than another. It means to live in the environment that one's society has deliberately chosen to construct (or to accept), and to do so rationally, self-consciously. This is what science makes available: the power and the knowledge to be effectual, to determine results, to control change. The knowledge of what is possible—an ever widening knowledge of ever new possibilities, and the technique of implementing these—this is modernity.

Not to change something when one might change it, given initiative and available resources, is tantamount to choosing the status quo; and we all choose what already exists far more than in present-day circumstances we are compelled to do. Modernity, I am contending, lies not in what one chooses but in the fact of being able to choose, even if one does not actually choose change or take advantage of potentialities.

Ignorance, then, is a bar to being modern. He who does not know what the twentieth century has made possible is not modern even when he in fact stands, though blindly, before rich alternatives. Awareness, plus technology—which is crystallized, materialized awareness—constitutes the basis of modernity.

The process of modernization then, I suggest, is that process by which a country becomes conscious of itself and of its processes, and of the kind of country that it is possible for it to become, and by which it finds or constructs the technical means for executing such choices as it consciously or unconsciously makes. Modernity in the world at large is in process of rendering feasible the gradual transformation of human life from what it has been into what we choose to make it. Our awareness that this is so, our choosing that we will strive for one thing rather than another (whatever the choice be; but it has to be made), and our ability to implement our decision technically—these are the measure of our being modern.

The responsibility is terrific; and the implications large.

6

Mankind's Religiously Divided History Approaches Self-Consciousness*

A cosmopolitanism about man's religiousness has become widespread and has made traditional theological attitudes obsolete, as we have already seen in the first selection in this anthology. What Smith demonstrates now is how relatively recent our present-day cosmopolitanism is. Not much more than a century ago, the West's conception of such an entity as "Buddhism" was vague at best; and the name "Hinduism," also coined in modern times, is a European rather than an Indian invention.

We have also observed already that Smith's 1963 book The Meaning and End of Religion *proposed abandoning the term "religions" in the plural, since in his view such usage allows the particular externals of religious traditions to distract the observer from an underlying, unifying quality of personal faith, and allows constructs of static religious systems to obscure the constantly changing flow of those externals. The other principal feature of* The Meaning and End of Religion *may now be indicated here: namely, Smith's analysis tracing historically the use of*

* Reprinted in slightly abridged form from *Harvard Divinity Bulletin* 29:1, 1–17. Copyright © 1964 by Wilfred Cantwell Smith. Used by permission.

the word "religion" and of the names of the individual "religions." What is said of the developing awareness of "Buddhism" in the present essay is of a piece with that larger inquiry.

The following hymn concluded the convocation of Harvard Divinity School on September 30, 1964:

> *Creation's Lord, we give Thee thanks,*
>   *That this Thy world is incomplete . . .*

> *That Thou hast not yet finished man;*
>   *That we are in the making still . . .*

> *Since what we choose is what we are,*
>   *And what we love we yet shall be,*
> *The goal may ever shine afar;*
>   *The will to win it makes us free.*

William DeWitt Hyde, 1903

It followed immediately on this essay of Smith's, which was his inaugural address as he took up his position at Harvard.

What does man's new cosmopolitanism about religious diversity portend for the future? The answer, in keeping with Smith's notion of the historical process and of modernity, will depend on the choices that the members of mankind's religious communities have yet to make. And the principal target of these remarks, clearly, was Christian leadership, on whose choices Smith may already have had some discernible effect.

*We are the products of our past, to be sure; but we are the producers of our future.—*ED.

It is the business of a university to discern and to clarify what is going on, inside a galaxy or a neuron, or indeed, in a religious community. Part of the excitement of academic inquiry is the constant discovery that more is going on than one might have supposed: that what seemed simple is complex; that what seemed static is in motion; that what seemed a disarray of brute facts is a sophisticated system of subtle interrelationships. Of the human situation it is the historian whose role it is to study the process of change, who has the privilege of detecting what has been and is going on—and the joy finally of seeing it, and letting it be seen by others, as intelligible. If the history of anything is the process by which it has come to be what it is, the historian is agog to know and to understand that process.

"To know and to understand": those are big words, and might sound arrogant, were it not that every advance in science, natural or humane, every discovery, of course raises more problems than it solves and introduces the intellect to realms of which it previously had not even known that it was ignorant. Yet this, though keeping one humble, does not diminish the delight each time of having found that the outer cover, at least, of this new challenge had proven intellectually manageable. To know and to understand are a university's legitimate and verified aspirations. And they are their own reward.

The plot, however, thickens; as we all know only too well. To get knowledge and understanding is good, but it is also consequential. Hiroshima is the vivid example. No one holds any longer that science affects man only superficially or externally; that a technological society, which means man's living in terms of his science, raises only technical questions. The moral, metaphysical, and religious issues that have been transformed by man's new understanding of the external world of nature are issues with which an educated audience is familiar. Similarly searching renovations of moral, metaphysical, and religious issues are induced by man's new awareness of history: mankind's new knowledge of the past and new understanding of it as a process and as one that is not "past," since as a process it is not yet over. The task of the historian is to provide an understanding of an earlier phase, or phases, of that continuing long-range process in the current phase of which man is today involved. Historians discover, and tell their fellows, that man has always been involved in process but they discover also that man has not always known this; today he does, and is beginning not only to know but to understand it.

At first, the awareness is disruptive. For the first effect is the negative one that old stabilities crumble, old patterns seem to dissolve. Presently, however, may follow a positive awareness of the not unintelligible dynamism within which one moves. A society that has begun to understand what it has been and is doing, has entered a profoundly new phase of its career.

My general point may be illustrated forcefully in the field of religious studies. The dislocation of much modern assurance, especially in the seminaries, came recently from the new awareness that the heritage, which had seemed fixed and stable, was in flux; and over against any feeling that ideally it ought to be fixed and stable, came the further awareness that it has always been in flux, from the very beginning (if any point in the continuum profits by being given that name). Research, especially historical research in its most comprehensive sense, has been revolutionizing understanding of the Old Testament and, most crucially, of the New Testament; of the Church in its on-going flexibility, or vitality; of theology, or may we perhaps say of theologizing; and indeed of everything that it touches. It is not merely our idea of the content of these that has been being radically revised, but our idea also of their form, and even of the notion that they have a form, in heaven at least if not on earth. The historian further notes that some while back, as an outcropping from the deposit of an earlier phase, it was felt apprehensively that to admit fluidity is to undermine, to call attention to it is unfriendly, to proclaim it is suicidal, or that the transient must be the peripheral, that that only is essential that persists immutable amidst subsidiary change. The historian kept relentlessly at work, however, and made it evident that by *this* reckoning everything was in process of becoming peripheral, that the "essential" was dwindling to insignificance.

Once the historical consciousness has become more fully appropriated, however, and interiorized, then the awareness of process can be liberating rather than dismaying, exhilarating rather than benumbing; and education becomes a training in a dynamic mankind's self-consciousness. One becomes not merely an affirmative, even joyous, participant in an ongoing evolution but, one hopes, a participant with a disciplined and clarified understand-

ing of the process in which one's Church or other society is involved, able therefore to participate intelligently, with self-critical, analytic awareness. The process-part of one's heritage, one
discovers, is not inimical to the heart of it, the ultimacy, the
value; the process *is* the heritage, so that the historian's function
is to attain and to purvey so true an appreciation of the process
that its self-conscious evolution from now on may be a worthy
but transcending extrapolation of its past.

If all here on earth is process, then the educated man is one
who knows this, who understands the process until now, and who
is equipped to participate intelligently—with critical intelligence, analytic but also (and this is faith) constructive.

A divinity school, especially in a university, is that organ of
the Church by which the Church becomes critically self-conscious
of its own evolution until now, and where it trains a minority of
itself to become leaders in that evolution from now on. Not only
the history department of a university, but to a significant degree
a whole faculty of arts, is that organ of a society by which the
society becomes self-conscious of *its* evolution until today, and
trains those of its members who are to execute its evolution next.
The rise of the natural sciences, with their spectacular success in
making possible mankind's growing understanding and control
of the objective world, is a prelude to the even more exhilarating
emergence now in sight of a self-consciousness of human history,
the potential rise of mankind's understanding and eventual direction of the process of its own development.

The prospect is exhilarating, but not encouraging: the first
indications would seem to portend disaster. We now all know
that a scientific control of objective nature may be used for destructive as well as for ameliorative purposes. It even seems that
destruction is somehow easier than amelioration. Similarly as
man becomes the conscious extrapolator of process, he is terrified
to realize how ill-equipped he is to play this role. We may bun-
gle, stupendously. We may lose nerve. Yet the dread and the
responsibility cannot annul the intelligence of nuclear fission
and fusion, once these have been attained; nor can they annul

the awareness of process. Can we learn to be wise participants in a process of whose past and present we are more and more intelligently aware and for whose future we are more and more inescapably responsible?

It is in answering these questions that the religious communities of the world are becoming more and more significantly involved. May one not add, that unless these questions are answered religiously, it seems increasingly unlikely that they will not be answered at all. In stressing human responsibility and awareness, I am not choosing the humanist side of a reason-*versus*-faith controversy, now outdated, but pleading for faith not over against process but in the midst of it.

For the religious quality of life, whatever it may have been in the past, is increasingly becoming that of living not apart from the historical process, not unaware of the process, not in other terms than process terms, but participating within the process fully and intelligently and also wisely, bravely, serenely, with that redeeming quality, characteristically human yet transcendent, that we inadequately call faith.

This is true for Christian or Hindu, Buddhist or Muslim.

Let us turn, then, to the question of our particular concern: the fact that mankind has been religious in a multiplicity of diverse ways, and in sharply separated groups. For the matter of that, Christendom itself has been Christian in a multiplicity of diverse ways; the Church is in process of becoming self-conscious on this point, and ecumenicity emerges as a theoretical or practical issue. Hindus have been religious in an even greater number of even more radically divergent ways, without apology; Muslims also have internal diversities, no doubt on a smaller scale but Buddhists again on a large one. And so on. Beyond these internal variations on each theme, however, human history evinces a plurality of themes. Not a vast plurality: there are a half-dozen or so major groups today, and all the minor ones put together constitute less than one further major group; and perhaps all the irreligious people in the world might be lumped together to constitute still another minority group, not without interest.

Mankind is religiously divided: that is a fact. Here I wish to consider a little our awareness of the fact, and the significance (and process) of that awareness. Let us look briefly at the comparative study of religion.

So far as the West goes, this study is recent. The modern story begins incipiently with the Age of Discovery, with Western Christendom reaching out to the rest of the world, probing, exploring, groping, gradually becoming aware of peoples and places far beyond its previous horizon. There were brought back accounts, weird or wonderful, of other men's "religions"—at first haphazardly, as travelers' tales, later in more ordered fashion and more abundantly. The nineteenth century saw the rise of a great attempt to give this matter serious and disciplined consideration: searching out material, recording it carefully, scrutinizing it systematically, interpreting it. This was the task of the universities, chiefly in Europe (though the North American continent has also begun, and characteristically in a somewhat new spirit).

There are, in my judgment, three levels in the comparative-religion task today; it is only a partial over-simplification to say that these correspond roughly to three stages in the Western historical development. I may label them information, interpretation, and generalization; or respectively the study of traditions, the understanding of faith, and the drawing of conclusions. Let us look at each in turn.

The acquiring of information did and must come first: the discovery, with increasing breadth and increasing precision, of what have in fact been the various religious traditions of mankind. This has involved the learning of languages, the establishment and dating of texts, the ascertaining of rituals and social structures, the accumulation and the analysis of endless data. Over the past one hundred fifty or one hundred years, much advance has been made in all this. The religious traditions of the world are becoming known, in their historical array. Most of us have, I think, an inadequately vivid notion of how great a change in Western consciousness has been wrought, for we can hardly imagine how ignorant the Western world recently was—

for instance, at the beginning of the nineteenth century. I found it very illuminating when I had occasion to examine the articles in this area in the various editions of the *Eycyclopaedia Britannica*. To take the Buddhist example: the fourth edition, 1810, has in its twenty big volumes no article on the Buddhist community or its religious tradition. The edition does refer in its article CHINA to a "sect of the idol FO," as a pernicious superstition introduced from India contaminating the (deistic) "purity" of the "ancient religion of China"; and it has also a brief entry FO, in five words: "an idol of the Chinese." Apparently one did not know, however, that FO was the Chinese designation for the Buddha. In the seventh edition, 1842, there is an article BUDDHA, "one of the two appearances of Vishnu," who is said to have appeared thus in order to mislead the enemies of the gods, inducing them to take up false opinions and to reject the Hindu religion and hence to be destroyed—which seems perhaps to reflect an Indian memory of a hated heresy. The eighth edition, 1853–61, under JAPAN recognizes "the religion of *Buddhu*" as one of the traditions of that country, and under CHINA there is at last mention of "all the follies and absurdities of the doctrines of Buddha" as having been brought in and grafted onto the superstitions of the Chinese. However, believe it or not, it is the ninth edition, 1875, before one finds an article BUDDHISM.

The Western world, then, has been moving from a position of ignorance to one of information on the religious traditions of those groups with whom it shares this planet. A doctoral student these days is flabbergasted to discover what an overwhelming mass of information has in fact now become available, on any *one* tradition. Moreover, the reference above to the distorted Indian memory of the Buddha may illustrate the point that Asia too has only recently begun to have at its disposal a serious and critical knowledge of its own past; and Africa, of course, is only now just beginning to get one. The Hindu has become historically concerned in serious fashion only very recently. It is true that Islamic and Chinese civilizations have been historiographic; yet even for them the awareness of process (for example, the

Muslim awareness that what they now call Islam has itself developed, has always been in transition) is modern—and revolutionary. The Afro-Asian awareness of the West, including the West's history, has been imposed upon it, again fairly recently. A knowledge and understanding within each Afro-Asian civilization of the others is only today beginning to be seriously and systematically pursued. Departments of comparative religion in Tokyo, Banaras, and Cairo are incipient—but may also prove revolutionary. Mankind is becoming aware of the massively multiform history of its religious life.

The second level of our studies, beyond the growing accumulation of information on diverse religious traditions, is the under-standing of personal faith. To this distinction between tradition and faith I give the greatest importance. By "tradition" you know, probably, what I mean: the doctrines, the legal institutions, the dance patterns, the art, the architectural constructions —anything that can be and is transmitted externally from one generation to another, that can be observed, and objectively established. By "faith," on the other hand, what do I mean? I do not intend to define it; one might be tempted to work on the operational definition that faith is what the tradition means— whatever it may mean—to the insider. The faith of a Buddhist is the meaning that the Buddhist tradition has for him, in its cosmic implications. If we think of an outsider studying the Church, for example, we can recognize that it is one thing for him to learn that in Christian worship there is a cross; it is another thing for him to ascertain what the cross means to the Christian who is worshiping. Something similar holds for other groups, other symbols, other ages. The first stage for the West, including the Church, was to learn what precisely have been and are the religious forms of the world's various communities. More recently we have begun to enter a phase of attempting to understand the significance of these forms in the religious life of those for whom they have been avenues of faith. (In the Orient, by the way, the matter has generally been the other way around: a certain appreciation of one's neighbour's faith has been somewhat devel-

oped, whereas a disciplined knowledge of other religious traditions is recent at best.)

To return to the West's incipient concern not only to know
outward form but to penetrate inner meaning: part of its new
understanding is the realization that the significance of the traditional forms for the man of faith reaches far beyond the religious
tradition itself, to embrace the whole of life—so that one should
perhaps say, rather, that faith is what the universe means to a
religious man, in the light of his tradition. We understand the
faith of Hindus only when, like them, we can use the religious
tradition of Hindus to enable us to see all of life, from medicine
to nuclear weapons, from economic development to the disloyalty
of a friend, through Hindu eyes.

No one need remind me that if the understanding of an outside tradition is exacting, the understanding of another faith is
difficult in the extreme; it has hardly begun. Even with the new
opportunities of asking those who hold it, the faith of other men
has hardly yet become intelligible. Muslims, for example, may
say what their tradition and its symbols mean to them, and yet
do so in terms that we on the outside cannot understand. One of
the characteristics of religious faith has been precisely that often
it can be spoken of meaningfully only to those within the same
tradition.

Some even have gone so far as to erect this into a final principle, that it is essentially impossible for an outsider to understand
a religious faith. "Only Christians can understand Christianity,"
it has been remarked; and only Muslims, Islam. Such a stand is
not ridiculous; the point is serious and must be given weight. It
is far too early, however, to accept it in the sense of agreeing
ahead of time that an understanding of the faith of other men is
totally impossible, and there is no use trying. I personally am
convinced that it can be done, even though I know that it is
difficult. Yet even those who are persuaded that the enterprise
will fail, should surely be willing to wait let us say one hundred
and fifty years, until we have applied as much energy and intellect to the attempt to understand faith as we have applied in the

last one hundred and fifty to attempt to understand traditions. If
at the end of that time we have got nowhere, *then* perhaps we
may call it off. In the meantime, the venture is far too exciting,
and the tentative results already beginning to accrue seem vastly
too promising, for such pessimism.

Nevertheless, let no one underestimate the gravity of our new
ambition: to understand a faith that we do not hope to share.
We leave aside for the moment a consideration of the revolutionary implications of this in case we should succeed—the attainment of a new type of religious outlook, the opening up of
perhaps a new chapter in mankind's religious history.

Our third heading is "generalization." After men have informed themselves on the historical facts of religious diversity,
and have learned to understand and appreciate the faith of other
men, what emerges? Is the intellect ready yet to induce some
general truths? Has one arrived at a stage to say something of
man's religiousness itself, of the fact of faith as a well-nigh universal human quality, immensely diversified in particular, remarkably persistent in general? Can one make any overall sense
out of so vast a panorama of data?

Attempts in these directions, formulations about the general
"nature of religion" and the like, have seemingly been encouraged by the growing awareness of man's variegated religious history, but curiously enough have also been curtailed by it. It is
empirical historical knowledge, in increasing sweep and detail,
that punctures speculative generalizations in this realm. The
historian has grown sufficiently well informed these days that to
even the most brilliant interpretations of the speculative theorist
he offers specific stark exceptions. Gone are the days when it was
possible for a Christian theologian, for example, to generalize
that all non-Christian religions are merely mundane human constructs, vacuous of any divine element to be found only within
the Church; or when it was possible for a Hindu universalist to
generalize that all religions are essentially the same; or for an
academic secularist to generalize that they are all sociological
opiates or derivatives of father fixations or any other one thing,

simple or complex. We simply know too much, historically, for any such generalizations to be convincing any more except to the ill-informed; or to the dogmatic, unable or unwilling to integrate their empirical knowledge and their religious beliefs. Apart from these superseded gross generalizations, even the more refined propositions of careful students are always liable to rebuttal by new empirical awareness.

We have also come to know too much, however, for isolationist thinking to be any longer adequate. The scope of our awareness has broadened so as to compel the "comparative study of religion": that is, taking seriously the relation of each religious community to the others, and to the whole. Whether of one's own community or of other peoples', such relations are now seen to be of major significance, both historically and otherwise.

This third level, generic understanding, it is now recognized, must be based squarely on the first two levels, historical knowledge and the understanding of specific groups. Certainly no one can understand man's religiousness in general who does not understand it in particular. And preferably, perhaps imperatively, in its particular diversity. At McGill, where I taught, we required as a precondition for admission to the doctorate in Comparative Religion that the candidate have the B.D. or M.A. or its equivalent, with the appropriate classical languages, in at least two differing traditions, of which one might well be his own. One cannot compare, unless one knows what one is comparing. So weighty is this point, that some have wondered how anyone can be so insensitive or obtuse or intellectually dishonest as to accept a post in comparative religion at all, since clearly no one can possibly these days know enough about the various "religions" at an academic level to compare them. I am sufficiently aware of the ever expanding field to feel more than most people could the force of this argument. Yet the principle works also the other way around. For our new awareness confirms that, as the old aphorism put it, to understand any religion, one must understand all. Not in addition to, but in some sense as part of, the task of understanding the tradition and the faith of each major

community, is the over-all task of understanding man's religiousness. There is something essentially false in the custom that has
grown up of proffering books on "The Religions of the World"
that present these in separate chapters, even by different authors,
one on Judaism, one on Hinduism, one on Shinto, and so on.
The question of how separate those chapters really are, is too
serious to let go by default. The relation among the parts is too
subtle and yet too important to be merely hinted at by the various chapters' simply being bound together into a single volume.

It is indeed overly bold, as I have cheerfully admitted, to pro-
fess comparative religion, modern knowledge on the various
traditions having grown too large for one man to command. Yet
the opposite is also true: our comparative knowledge today is
such, that one might ask how anyone can dare to talk about any
one religious expression, if his understanding of it is limited by a
failure to see it in a global perspective, an inability to bring to
bear on it a comprehensive insight that can appreciate it within
the total context of man's religiousness itself in all its polymor-
phic sweep.

The fact is that no one should talk about other men's faith
with confidence. The Trappist tradition of silence is a standing
rebuke to *all* of academia. Yet the answer to this is intellectual
humility, not self-satisfied specialization.

For it is beginning to be possible to see that an attempt to
study Islam in itself is inadequate: that what in fact one is studying is the Islamic strand in a world religious complex, the Islamic strand in the history of man's religiousness. The awareness
of this is today more accessible to outside students than to Muslims themselves, but in both cases it is growing. Among the
former it is important; among the latter it will be revolutionary.
In the Christian case, Christians themselves are in the revolution,
are increasingly conscious that to understand their religious development accurately is to see it within a wider context. The Old
Testament used to be understood as an item in itself, but is
increasingly seen as more truly understandable when viewed
within the total evolution of the religious complex of the ancient

Near East; and even the New Testament similarly, in a way that the Church has hardly yet found an adequate way to formulate; to say nothing of the early history of the Church [For a discussion written later, progressing from the Bible's historical context to its historical influence as a scripture, see Chapter 3 above.—ED.].

It has certainly been true for some time now and for considerable parts of the world that men have lived their life religiously in independent, even isolationist, communities, separated from each other not absolutely, of course, but in principle, and even considerably so in practice. Our new study of mankind's religiousness, however, is investigating the fact that this situation arose in human development. In *The Meaning and End of Religion* I have suggested that it arose at a given time and place—in Western Asia, in that fascinatingly creative period between Alexander and Muhammad—and has since established itself, and has spread, though not to all the world: to India quite late, and to China virtually never. We in the West have come to take it so utterly for granted that religious life should be lived out in separated and boundaried communities, that we have given less attention than it deserves to the great question of how this came to be and what it implies. Yet one is beginning to discern perhaps a total history of man's religiousness, constituting a pattern in which the rise of the separated religious communities constitutes a meaningful episode, within the total pattern. I personally have begun to think that I discern in the role of the Manichees an illuminating link in the total story of man's religious development, a piece that may lock together into a perhaps coherent total picture the Hindu, Buddhist, and Chinese pieces and the Parsi, Jewish, Christian, and Islamic pieces. I may well be wrong on this, and I myself am aware of difficulties, but it has struck me that the investigation is worth pursuing.

However that may be, and indeed whatever we may eventually find the past history of religious separation to have been, there remain the present and the future. I am profoundly persuaded that mankind, all over the globe, is today in process of entering a significantly new phase in the religious history of the world. On

this a few things, at least, are clear. The first is that that history is
not yet over; and of course, that that history will be different in
the future from what it has been in the past. Something profound, something very profound indeed, is happening within the
two communities that I know at closest range, the Christian and
the Muslim. I think it almost impossible to exaggerate the radical nature of the transformation that is discernibly in process.
And although I speak more superficially in their cases, yet, so far
as I am able to discern, the other religious traditions of mankind
also, the Jewish, the Hindu, the Buddhist, are not static.

Quite misleading is the prevalent dichotomizing picture of the
contemporary Asian choosing between his religion, given in fixed
form by the past, and modernity, also pretty much given in a
fixed form by the West. In fact what the Asian is choosing
among, less or more consciously but with growing awareness as
time goes on, is a series of potential religious futures, no one of
which is given, no one of which can be thought of as untinged by
modernity. The future of Hindus will be Hindu, in an unrecog-
nized form yet to be created; the future of Buddhists will be
Buddhist, not in any past sense but in some future one; the
future of the Muslim world will be the next, novel chapter in the
religious history of an Islamic evolution now vigorously in process.

We do not know enough yet to say with assurance that what is
happening in each of the traditions is comparable to what is
happening in all the others in anything but scope and depth. Yet
even within the boundaries of each tradition, the effect of the
new and growing knowledge of man's religious history until now
is increasingly relevant. A religious tradition lies behind each
man's personal faith; but a consciousness of that tradition in its
fully historical quality is a new ingredient in the religious life of
man. In each case those who used to see themselves as carriers of
a pattern now know that instead they, or shall I say we, are
participants in a process. Moreover, the consciousness of the process of one's own tradition is becoming supplemented increasingly, at least among leaders, by a consciousness of the processes

of the traditions of other men. Throughout the world, each of the major religious communities of mankind is beginning to be conscious of itself as within the context—the developing context —of the others. The next chapter of the history of the religious life of men on this planet will be written by men aware of this total context.

These men are certainly aware of each other. Whether we like it or not, and as a matter of fact most of us do like it, at least at this level religious isolationism is coming to an end. To take one illustration: Presbyterians nowadays are reading Methodist books. Both are reading Buber—and Radhakrishnan. Tillich is being read in Tokyo. And I know of a Muslim critique of Karl Barth.

These men will be aware also, and increasingly, of the growing practical unification of mankind. The question is pointedly asked whether the various religions are a divisive or a unifying force in our shrinking world. The more searching question, not least for the participant, is again one of becoming. How is the development of one's own religious tradition (and ultimately also that of others) to move in such a way that it may contribute more effectively to world community? Not: What is the role of each community in establishing compatibility, collaboration, and brotherhood? Rather: What, through penitence and faith, may it become?

This is the significant question both for us who are academic historians, and for those of us who have a vision of world brotherhood, which we believe to be a step towards God's vision. It is perhaps a tiny yet growing minority of Muslims who have come to feel that the truth of Islam may lie not so much in the past as in the future. With Christians I would argue that the truth of the Church for us lies in what the Church should become during this particular phase of its process that God has entrusted to our hands. With my fellow social scientists I would argue that to understand the current dynamic towards mankind's global integration and its frustrations requires *inter alia* a fuller understanding than we now have of the processes of the various religious communities' becoming quickly or haltingly aware of, and taking seriously or shirking, their involvement in that dynamic.

I do not know how theologians will deal with the questions that our new awareness of mankind's religious diversity poses. I do know, however, that these questions will now be among those with which in one way or another they must deal. And not only the Christian theologian: Jewish and Buddhist and Hindu religious leaders also will from now on be increasingly aware, and be leading communities increasingly aware, of not only their own but also the total religious history of mankind.

I am ready to argue with a Christian theologian, on Christian premises, that the modern comparative religionist's vision of the religious history of mankind provides a truer vision of that total history—that is, a vision closer to God's way of seeing it, a more authentic *Heilsgeschichte*—than is any interpretation of this wide-ranging matter formulated within the Church in the days before the present information, or indeed any serious historical information, was available. It is significant to add this: that I would argue the corresponding point with Muslim theologians, on Islamic premises. I also assert that a true understanding of Islamic religious history will be not of Islam itself but of the Islamic strand in the world's religious complex. I write that sentence not glibly, but in full seriousness, realizing that the radically new vision that it implies would have to be defended before and ultimately assimilable by Muslims themselves. And Muslim members of my audience are themselves a portent of the new world situation in which religious discourse is being carried on. I can sense that they too may be restless at what seems my humanist heresy, like some of us Christians; but in both cases my answer would be that this religious reconceptualization is not simply my wish but is necessitated by the advance of modern knowledge. Muslim theologians too will be discussing for the next few generations the theological significance of their own and their community's new awareness of mankind's global religious development, their own and other peoples'.

This brings us, then, to a point where we can answer finally the question that we raised about general truths arising from our new awareness. The classical query, what do the various religions of the world have in common, can now be given a new answer. It is, indeed, a new *type* of answer: historical rather than formally philosophic, dynamic rather than absolutist, having to do with becoming rather than being. Also, it is a personalist answer, having to do primarily with men rather than primarily with systems (since systems change, and it is men that change them). For first of all, what the various religious traditions have in common is the fact that each is being carried today by persons who increasingly are involved in the same problems. Christians, Jews, Buddhists, Hindus, Muslims, and the others are all facing today, for the first time, by a joint challenge: to collaborate in building a common world. This must be not only the kind of world in which we can all live together, but the kind also of which we can jointly approve, and to the building and sustaining of which the faith of each can effectively inspire. I have said that this is an historical rather than a formally philosophic answer to the question; but I suggest that it will growingly prove itself to be more cogent, more revolutionary, more spiritually penetrating than any doctrinal universalism. I have suggested this viewpoint on other occasions, however, and will not develop it further here.

Secondly, it has been remarked that the most important thing that two religious communities can have in common is a clear and mutually agreed awareness of their differences. This is a penetrating insight, the profundity and consequences of which will only gradually be recognized as, superseding misunderstanding, we begin to act on it, for instance in Catholic-Protestant and Jewish-Christian encounter. I would elaborate it, to say that religious communities throughout the world have just begun to set forth on the unimaginably promising venture of becoming authentically aware of each other, and of themselves in relation to each other, and all in relation to the unending process of transition of which we have spoken and through which each is living. Among all religious communities throughout the world there is a growing common awareness for the first time not only of the world in which we live (given by science), but also of the total process of the whole religious history of man, stretching back now at least 100,000 years, evincing fantastic variety, continual evolution, sharp and at times rigid separations, and today entering a new phase in all its parts.

I am not suggesting that distinctions will dissolve. I am suggesting, rather, that those distinctions will survive that men wittingly choose to maintain.

In fine, what the religious communities of the world have in common is an increasingly common awareness of their past, in all its dynamic variety, and an increasingly common involvement in and shared responsibility for an increasingly joint future. We—men on earth—are just now beginning to understand ourselves in our diversity, to understand the long centuries of our past religiousness in all its variety, to understand the present in its continuing variety but its gradual closing in of intercommunication, and to establish the intellectual self-consciousness in which we as human beings on earth shall in the future with increasing deliberateness and renewed reverence construct the future history of our religious life.

It is an exhilarating task, and an awesome one.

To use the language of faith: God has called us to serve Him (and our fellows) along ways lofty, untrodden and precarious, yet not forbidding. To Him be the praise.

PART THREE

Religious Diversity and Mutuul Understanding

7

Participation: The Changing Christian Role in Other Cultures*

A theme which unites the last three essays in this collection may be termed mutual understanding. The choice of these words is not especially Smith's indeed, he offers much less of an attempt at a systematic, philosophical discussion of a notion of "understanding" than have a number of other scholars in the comparative-religion field— but it can be argued that the other word, "mutual," points close to the center of his thought and intent.

The word "mutual" is useful because it enables us to group together the justifications Smith proposes for his views in addressing the three distinct audiences of the next three essays. From this essay's quite pragmatic proposals to the Christian missionary enterprise, we shall move to comparative-religion scholarship in the next selection, and then to interdisciplinary inquiry in the university at large in the following. Yet despite these disparate applications, mutual understanding is throughout for Smith an imperative with moral as well as intellectual qualities: the type

* Reprinted in slightly abridged form from *Occasional Bulletin* of the Missionary Research Library, New York, 20:4 (April, 1969) 1–13. Also published in *Religion and Society* 18:1 (1970), 56–74. Copyright © 1970 by Wilfred Cantwell Smith. Used by permission.

*of discourse which is to be sought is what promotes community
among men. "Understanding," as I read Smith's references to it,
is not comprehension alone; it should be distinctly colored with
shades of sympathy, if not outright agreement.*

*Smith's audience for this essay was the biennial convention of
the Division of Overseas Ministries of the National Council of
Churches, representing the mission leadership of the principal
American Protestant denominations, meeting in New Haven,
November 21, 1968. His remarks represent a direct address to
Christian missionary thinking to move forward from the unpro-
ductive situation described in our first selection, "The Christian
in a Religiously Plural World" (1961). By the mid-sixties, the
winds of openness and change had quickened considerably,
notably with the Second Vatican Council and the consequent
extension of the ecumenical movement to include Catholic as
well as Protestant and Orthodox Christendom. Various sorts of
dialogue had become fashionable, and the suggestion had begun
to be canvassed that there was no reason a truly ecumenical spirit
should stop at Christian frontiers. And in the years since 1968,
the imperative for community has remained even in the face of
renewed particularist trends in various quarters. There may be
grounds for hope that the mutual efforts which Smith envisions
in this essay may flourish.—ED.*

I

In "participation," I would venture to suggest, we may have a
theme that could prove serviceable in the cause of missionary
thinking for our day. This concept may provide a helpful new
way of looking at the role of the missionary; and indeed, if this
does not sound too pretentious, perhaps also at the whole modern Christian, and human, religious enterprise.

Perhaps I may lead us into the subject via the same route that
I myself traveled over the years in reaching it: namely, with a
consideration of the Islamic instance. I began with the usual
notion that Islam was the name of a religion, the religion that

Muslims have or, more sensitively, aspire to have. I then devoted a good part of twenty years to a fascinating and delightful and rewarding search for an understanding of Islam. I had the good fortune to live in a Muslim community, to have many Muslim friends; and a good part of the zest of that search for understanding derived from the fact that many of my Muslim friends, mostly intellectuals but some of them also gradually getting into active positions of responsibility, were also engaged in such a search. Theirs was no academic or purely theoretical quest, but a serious wrestling with the issue of what is God's will in the novel, perplexing, ever changing world of our twentieth century. What does it mean, they were concerned to know, to be a Muslim in the challenging vicissitudes of modern life and thought? Beyond their classical heritage from the past, with its historical approximations and deviations, its good and its bad and its developments—and amid the welter of modern interpretations, by no means unanimous—what is true Islam?

My studies over the years were reasonably vigorous and always entrancing. They were the studies of an outside observer yet one not totally outside, and certainly not dispassionate. I was pursuing an answer to the question of what Islam *is*: a resonant and haunting question, certainly a religious question, and for Muslims a cosmic one. In the course of that pursuit I found myself with increasing material for answering the rather different question as to what Islam has been. This latter is an historical matter including, of course, contemporary history, where it becomes the fascinating and marvelously important question of what, today, Islam is in process of becoming, on its mundane human side. There was also the recognition that my Muslim friends, as persons, were not captured within any forms.

To reduce what Islam is to what Islam has been, or is in process of becoming, as some outsiders, but no Muslims, have been tempted to do, would fail to recognize its religious quality: the relationship to the divine, the transcendent element. Indeed, Islamic truth must necessarily transcend Islamic actuality.

Nonetheless, for all its transcendence, even that higher Islam, in Muslims' hearts or just beyond their reach, on investigation turned out to have had a history. It has changed, and still changes. It has been different things in different centuries, in different countries, among different strata. It has been not a system but a flowing stream.

It turns out that the situation has in fact been across the ages what both their theologians and ours have always said was the case: namely, that religion is a response to a divine initiative. Islam has been a human activity, and even the Muslim's ideal of Islam has been an evolving human vision. Islam has been not a *purely* human activity, since it would not have been what it has been at any given moment if those involved in it had not at that moment seen more in it than that; and yet, for all that, it has been human, and an activity. Islam has been something that people do. And since those people have all been different, and living in varying places and times, it has been variegated and dynamic, a living tradition.

Islamic history has been and continues to be a divine-human complex. Like Christian history, it is still history: fluid, imperfect, creative, dynamic. It is divine-human encounter in motion. Muslims have been discovering this, as their historical awareness has grown, and especially also as they have gained political and other independence of late, and have once again, and indeed with new vitality, become self-consciously responsible for directing their own affairs. The establishment of Pakistan, for instance, gave that particular group of Muslims a cherished opportunity to guide their corporate lives in accord with Islam. This in turn made inescapable and specific and personal a wrestling with the question of what Islam is, deontologically—which is an Islamic way of saying, what is right and proper, cosmically; what is the Good, what is Justice, what is Truth.

Moreover, things have moved with sufficient swiftness that perceptive Pakistani Muslims have discovered in current events the fluidity, including religious fluidity, that the perceptive historian has been discovering in his new and sophisticated understanding of the heritage from the past: namely, that where they used to think of themselves as bearers of a pattern, they now realize that, rather, they are participants in a process.

II

We come, thus, to our key concept. For we have used here the word "participant" for the first time. And I hope that you can see the magnitude and the seriousness of what I am suggesting. To be a Muslim *means*, to participate in the Islamic process. And this is not merely an historical or sociological observation, although it is those; it is also a theological asseveration, ultimate, cosmic. It is also (but in the end delete "also") the only statement of what it means to be a Muslim, I suggest, on which both Muslims and outsiders might agree.

It is true at the most casual level: to be a Muslim, even for the nominal, the marginally pious, the insouciant, the heretic, the debonair, is to participate in the historical-cultural-social Islamic complex. And complex it is: it may mean to wear one kind of dress, to talk one kind of language, in Indonesia, and to wear different clothes, to speak a different tongue, even in some degree to believe (or to fail to believe) slightly different doctrines, to observe or to flout slightly different legal-moral traditions, in another area. For good or ill, and with wide latitude for regional and personal variation, even personal reaction, to be a Muslim is to participate somewhere in our twentieth-century phase of that elaborate Islamic process in the world whose past history is given, whose present vitality is open, whose future it is the willing or unwitting role of the participants in part to determine.

This is true for every Muslim, however secular we may call him or he may call himself. The casual, the willful, the destructive Muslim participates casually, willfully, destructively. At a more serious, more pious, more deeply involved level, to be a Muslim is to participate self-consciously, and responsibly, in the ongoing religious heritage and process of Islam. However conservative or radical such a Muslim may be, whether the past tradition elicits from him blind allegiance, or warm affection, or critical assessment, or reforming zeal, or motivating drive, or emulative aspiration, the religious Muslim too is that man who participates, deliberately, piously, joyously, in the Islamic religious stream.

At the highest mystical level, also, to be a Muslim (as distinct from being a Christian mystic or a Buddhist or a Hindu one) is to have communion with God through participation in the forms and patterns, channeled through the poetry and institutions, that constitute on earth the historical process of the specifically Islamic peoples.

"Do unto others as you would that they should do unto you" is an injunction that we have on the highest authority. In the comparative study of religion, I have found it a good rule to suggest for the interpretation of others' religious affairs only such theories and interpretations as may be applicable, or at the least intelligible, for one's own case. So far as this particular Islamic instance is concerned, I have chosen it only to illustrate a principle of, I submit, universal validity. To be a Buddhist means, similarly, something that it has traditionally been almost despondently impossible to define, so ebullient and unrestrained has been among Buddhists the variety of historical development. Yet all variety, all creativity, all seriousness are subsumed if one interprets it as meaning to participate religiously in the historical Buddhist movement, which began 2,500 years ago in northeast India and surged forth over much of Asia and much of the world since, and is still surging, is still creative. Again, "to be a Christian," I am happy enough both to propose for others and to accept for myself, means to choose to participate in the Christian Church: to take on its past, not without criticism, yet, for all its aberrations, without ultimate embarrassment; to take on its present, again certainly not without criticism, not without tears, but in the end also not without hope; to contribute what one can to its future, in full seriousness and responsibility and yet leave the outcome to God.

The freedom of the gospel is infringed if, legislatively, anyone declares to me that to be a Christian means to believe some particular thing, to join some particular organization, to observe some particular pattern, to formulate my highest aspirations and loyalties in terms of some particular images. Any specifically predicating definition would imprison me; or if I propounded one, if not open-ended, it would imprison others or offend them. Yet neither am I willing, no matter how stormy the chaos of change, to say that "to be a Christian" has no significant content. Those of us who plunge into the tumults of the present with a grateful, if sober, acceptance of the past tradition, instructive but not binding, may call ourselves Christians with full humility, full freedom, full commitment. We choose to participate in the historical Christian process because through it we find God—more strictly speaking, of course, because through it God finds us. Because of its history over the ages, and through its institutions inherited from the past and currently being overhauled, through its images, its doctrines, its foibles, its shortcomings, and its splendours, and through its community both of saints and of other sinners like ourselves, God finds us and calls us to serve Him and His world.

To be a Christian means to participate in the Christian process, just as to be a Muslim means to participate in the Muslim process; to be a Hindu, in the Hindu; and so on, and on. My own considered view, and I am prepared to argue for it against attack both from the right and from the left, is that each of these processes has been and continues to be a divine-human complex. To fail to see the human element in any would be absurd; to fail to see the divine element in any would be obtuse.

To put the matter in another way (and this will sum up our argument thus far): the historian, looking out over the history of the world, sees what used to be called the various religions—including his own—as a series of historical processes wherein the several religious communities on earth have been carrying out *sub specie aeternitatis* the ongoing task over the centuries of extrapolating for each age as it has come along the particular tradition inherited from its own past.

To be Christian or Muslim or Buddhist, to be religious, is a creative act, of participation in a community in motion.

III

The next step in the argument has to do with interrelationships. We note that these divers movements proceed not in water-
tight independence of each other, but at times in some sort of
mutual interaction. The degree of separateness and independence has varied at different times and places. I have been involved in a graduate seminar which has studied selected moments in human history where it would seem to be the case that
the interdependence and inter-involvement of two or more religious histories has been markedly greater than usual. One such
moment was the trilogue in mediaeval Spain; another was the
curious commingling of the *san chiao* (the "Three Teachings,"
or so-called "Three Religions") in mediaeval China; another,
bhakti devotion in sixteenth- and seventeenth-century India.

An illustration from the present, from modern India, of the
kind of thing that I mean has interested me. When in 1947 the
subcontinent was divided and Pakistan set up, the sizable Muslim community "left behind" in predominantly Hindu India
began a history of its own that has become in part separate from
and somewhat, though of course not entirely, independent of, the
neighbouring history of the Muslim community in Pakistan. Its
history, including its religious history, has also been in part dependent on, has been involved with, the religious evolution of
the Hindu community in India. Its status as a minority is somewhat precarious. Besides, its internal relation has been quite special to such time-honoured religious questions in the Islamic
world as the role of law (*shari'ah*) in community life, relations to
the state, and the like. Now in part the future of the Muslims in
India manifestly turns on the treatment accorded to them by the
Hindu majority. And this in turn depends in part upon the play
of two contending forces within the Hindu community, both of
age-long standing and both powerful.

These two strands in the Hindu religious complex, of divergent consequence, are conspicuous: we may call them particularist and universal. The one stresses rigidity of form, especially

social form, the closed cohesion of introvert community, separateness, and social distance; it is exemplified in the caste system
and cultivated these days by such communalist groups as the Jan
Sangh and the Rashtriya Sevak Sangh. The other emphasis from
the Hindu heritage is of liberal humanism, a powerful philosophic and spiritual orientation that stresses tolerance of human
diversity, openness of mind and heart, a profound respect for the
human spirit even across social boundaries, and the cosmic validity of all forms of worship. Now both these tendencies in the
Hindu community are, as I have said, ancient, deep, and powerful. Both are active today. Which will win out, or how the two
will balance or accommodate each other, are questions that may
well prove highly consequential not only for the history of India,
but perhaps also for the history of the rest of us. In any case, it is
clear that what happens in the present-day development of
Hindu thought and feeling in this regard will be highly relevant
for the evolution of Islamic affairs in India, including religious
affairs. The destiny of the two groups is sufficiently intertwined
that the religious development of the one will in part affect the
religious development of the other, whether by sympathy or by
reaction.

Here we have a fascinating example of the fact that sometimes
what happens in the historical process of one religious tradition
is a function of what happens in the historical process of another.
This kind of thing can be discerned, too, in past history and for
other communities, more often and more crucially than we usually recognize.

Another example of this same general point may be taken from
closer to home. To return to our "participation" language:
Marx, Darwin, and Freud have participated, not quite unwittingly, in the history of Christian theology. The religious history
of the Christian world, and more narrowly of the Christian
Church, and more narrowly still of Christian theology, liturgy,
institutional structure, and much else, has been impinged upon,
obviously, by the activities of many sorts of persons: not only by
the doings of scientists and technologists and urban planners and
non-planners, both within the Church and without it, but also

by specifically religious thinking and feeling and vision of men of another community. It has been said that the most important disciple of Mahatma Gandhi so far in the twentieth century has been Martin Luther King. In this among other ways Gandhi may be said to have participated consequentially in the Christian life of the United States.

The use of the term "influence" used to be the standard method of describing and analysing this kind of process. In the Middle Ages, Muslim and Jewish thinkers such as al-Ghazzali, Ibn Rushd ("Averroes"), and Maimonides participated, though largely unwittingly, in the formation of Christian Scholastic theology. And indeed Aristotle has played so fundamental a role in the process of Christian thought that we have forgotten even to be awed by it.

Another, more pejorative, term was "syncretism." I suggest that it too is inadequate to handling what has been going on, especially when one recalls that the reaction may be strongly negative. Karl Barth, to take a different kind of example, was "influenced" by men against whom he reacted creatively, so that his thought, though not understandable historically without their thinking as a foil from which he recoiled, yet transcended theirs. This was certainly not syncretism, and not merely influence; yet they participated in the formation of that new phase of Christian theology that Barth, for better or worse, initiated.

We may go further, however, and remark on a more intimate, two-way involvement. The kind of role-playing that I have hitherto instanced might be characterized as impersonal, and passive; some might argue that to call it "participation" is an exaggeration, since it was perhaps the writings and ideas of the persons, but not the persons themselves, that affected Christian history, and only to the point that that history was receptive. There is another level of involvement, however, that is more dialectically integrated, more dynamic. This is the level where men of other faith participate "live," as it were—deliberately, engagedly, and engagingly—in the transitions through which constructive religious thought is always going. They talk back, talk with, plan together, work together, think together, invited and inviting.

The term "dialogue" has been employed to designate a formalization of this, and one would hardly deny that this is potentially a striking emergence in Church and especially missionary policy, particularly if it becomes genuine and serious and substantial, not merely formal. Yet the more significant development is perhaps less structured and more active, in the day-to-day give-and-take of intellectual and social collaboration or, at the institutional level, in the new religion departments in liberal arts faculties in which Christians and representatives of several religions increasingly collaborate in the formation of ideas and interpretations and attitudes, and out of which at least one element in the next period of Christian religious history will manifestly come.

We are just at the beginning of a phase in Western religious evolution in which the role of Asian missionaries, Buddhist and Hindu and Muslim, and certainly of Buddhist and Hindu and Muslim ideas, and motifs in art, is evidently going to be consequential in the development of Christian life in one way or another. Few of us would care to predict what is likely to happen as a result; few, I guess also, would predict that nothing at all will. The missionaries may make some "converts," in the frontier-crossing, proselytizing sense of that term, although this is not the goal of, for instance, the Ramakrishna Mission. The category that I am proposing is that whereby, in one fashion or another, for good or ill, wittingly or unwittingly, little or much, Muslims, Hindus, and Buddhists may be seen as participating in the future evolution of the Western religious tradition. Whether we applaud or not, the Christian Church will become what it will become, Christian theology will develop into what it will develop into, Christian worship will take the form that it will take, in part as a result of their involvement in our affairs.

IV

Only at this third stage in our exposition do we come explicitly to the missionary. We are now ready to define the missionary as that man who deliberately sets out to participate in the history of another community. If he be a medical or educational or technical missionary, then his participation is in the mundane sector of that community's evolution. Yet neither he nor we nor they are so naïve or so dichotomizing as to suppose that the mundane history is not relevant to the religious, and vice versa; that the medical or educational or technical changes that he may introduce have no spiritual overtones or undertones. *A fortiori*, the more evangelical or theological, or in any way self-consciously theoretical, missionary is participating more directly in the cultural—that is, the religious—dimension of the community among whom he works, even if no more explicitly.

I have spoken of the missionary as a deliberate participant, since the rest of us also participate, often in spectacularly consequential ways. The degree to which Western ideas, techniques, institutions, and processes are transforming the history, including the religious history, of the rest of the world as well as of ourselves is obvious, even if frightening. The Wall Street banker and the Pentagon planner, as well as the technological innovator in agricultural machinery in Moscow or the American Midwest, are of course playing a role in the religious history of the Islamic and the Hindu and the Buddhist movements, however unconsciously and however ineptly.

Even at the cultural level, however, and even at that of strictly religious ideas, a Westerner knowingly or carelessly may significantly affect religious thought and practice, sensibility and concern, in Asia. Theodor Herzl is clearly an eminently significant figure in Islamic history. A Toynbee or a Tolstoy has been consequential in not only Christian throught. At a more homely level, any local citizen who invites an Asian student on a local campus into his home, or fails to invite him, may thereby turn out to be playing some small role in the religious evolution of Asia. Human history, including its religious history, is an intricate and delicate web of human relationships.

Let us return to the missionary who deliberately and conspicuously and flatly plants himself down in the midst of an alien community and sets about explicitly to set religious changes in motion. It is fairly easy to contend that even in the nineteenth century, and even though he was not aware of it, in actual historical fact the chief consequence of the presence of the Christian missionary in Asia was the role that he played in the religious history of the non-Christian world.

His participation was unwitting, and uncouth. So gawky was his intrusion, often, that the primary and at times explosive consequence was one of vehement reaction and antithetic rebound. There was also a positive role, perhaps particularly in the case of the mission colleges, where his participation in Asian history opened new horizons, elicited new aspirations and new motivations, which presently became incorporated within the ongoing religious traditions in the lands concerned. The role of C. F. Andrews in the life of Gandhi is one striking illustration. An instance of a quite different emergence is the Ramakrishna Mission, now important as a Hindu influence in the United States and elsewhere; its form certainly, and some of its content, it could be argued, are historically to be explained in terms of Christian missionary activity. (That does not mean that they are any less Hindu, but only that the participation was to that extent effective.)

The consequences were sometimes in line with, and sometimes in strident resistance to or in recoil from, what was being intended; yet whatever form they took, the fact remains that the historical consequences of the introduction of Christian missionary endeavour into the development of the other communities may be conceptualized most truly, I submit, in terms of their function within the indigenous religious movements of the Orient.

Of course, the ideological framework within which most of the missionaries then operated, and the groups in the West that sent them, was to an extreme degree individualistic. It is difficult now for any of us to imagine how utterly it was presupposed at that time that an individual person could be shifted, like a brand snatched from the burning, out of one sociological and cultural and historical complex and incorporated into another (the proselytizing process by which "a Muslim" or the like became "a Christian"), without any thought being given to sociological, institutional, economic, psychological, religious-historical, and other ramifications of such radical displacement. Of course, no one can weigh in a scale the eternal destiny of a single soul against the mundane dislocation of a million persons, and I do not wish to become involved in a theological argument as to the cosmic validity or significance of an individual conversion. All I would say on this point is that the proselytizing process too may most fruitfully be envisaged as an act by which an individual person chooses no longer to participate in the historical religious tradition and community in which he was brought up, but to participate instead in another one. This is what inter-community conversion is. (There is another sort of conversion, to which we shall come presently: conversion *within* one's own community and tradition.)

However that may be, the over-all number of outward conversions was small. So far as observable consequences in this world are concerned, the nineteenth-century Christian missionary movement's role in the religious history of the planet is to be measured and conceptualized primarily, I am suggesting, in terms of the playing of a role in the history of one tradition by intruders, or shall we simply say participants, from another. And in the twentieth century, or at least this latter part of it with our new understanding both of what we are doing and of what Muslims, Hindus, and Buddhists have been and are doing, I suggest thet the role of the Christian missionary may become self-consciously what it has always been in fact.

The theological question then becomes: What is the truly Christian role that a participant may play in the evolution of another culture? It would take me too far afield, and doubtless also be too controversial, to try a theological answer to that. I shall merely mention in passing my own conviction that the correct theological answer, given our new understanding, could mean a Christian missionary who was not merely a deliberate but also a joyous, and not merely a joyous but also a welcome, participant in the religious history of the rest of mankind.

The idea of a missionary being religiously "welcome," even invited, is strange, so accustomed has one grown to the notion that a Christian missionary is plotting to undermine and to destroy the religious processes in which those to whom he goes have been participating. That this should be so is an index of our stupefaction. I would affirm it as a basic principle, worthy of all credence, and of all new policy decisions, that no missionary is worth his salt unless what he has to say is welcomed by the leaders of the group among whom he works, so that they want to hear more; and if he is talking at the religious level, then he must be welcomed by the religious leaders.

Does this sound "far out" and ludicrously romantic? Am I dreaming about something far into the future? By no means; this stage has in fact already been reached. Only, on the whole it is happening under auspices other than those of the traditional missionary boards, and sometimes perhaps it is hardly even noticed by them that this in fact is where the action is. For Tillich is being read in Tokyo, Buber in Boston, and Aurobindo in Oxford. Radhakrishnan, as Hendrik Kraemer correctly pointed out, is virtually an apologist for the Hindu orientation; yet we invite him to Harvard Divinity School because we want to hear what he has to say. D. T. Suzuki was invited (*sic*) to participate (*sic*) in the life and thought of Union Theological Seminary in New York, and was welcomed there. Tillich was welcomed in Tokyo and is studied assiduously by Buddhists, because Buddhists hope that he will be able, as a Christian, to throw light on Buddhists' problems. These hopes are not absurd; neither are they disappointed.

My salient example is one of the most successful, as well as one of the most admirable, as well as one of the most welcomed, interfaith participants of the modern age: Martin Buber. Here was a Jew, profoundly Jewish, who had something to say to Christendom, and said it. Christians agreed that he had something to say, and read him studiously and with profit. They learned from him, or should we, rather, say learned through him, about God, about themselves, about the Christian tradition in which they were participants. They welcomed him, applauded

him, asked him to come back to give them more. I nominate
Martin Buber as the model of the modern missionary *par excellence*.

But, you may reply, he was not preaching Judaism, not trying
to convert, not trying to dominate. Of course not; and this, indeed, is precisely the point. He was not trying to dominate, and
the Christian Church must repent in dust and ashes for the
domineering, aggressive element in that phase of the Christian
missionary movement that is now, as we know, or may hope,
virtually at an end. He was not trying to proselytize, that is; it is
legitimate to use the word "convert" in that other sense in which
every true Christian hopes to be truly converted every morning:
namely, to be converted more closely, and still more closely, to
God and to the truth. In this sense many of us have been converted, again and again, by Buber, into being Christians of truer
piety. He was not preaching Judaism; and by the same token it is
a sorry evangelist, as the fundamentalists have long since known,
who does not know the meaning of the aphorism "We are not
preaching Christianity: we are preaching Christ."

The counterpart today to the issue in the early Church about
circumcision and the Jewish law is the question of baptism and
church membership. The first Christians had to face a question
which we could phrase: "Does acceptance of the good news mean
that he who accepts it must become a member of our Jewish
community? Must he participate in our process?" The answer
"yes" was given, but fortunately the answer "no" prevailed. The
modern counterpart question is: "Does what God has to offer to
the world through the Christian Church entail others' opting for
participation in our religious history?" Let us hope that the missionary wing of the Church will not be the last section of it to
recognize that here too the answer most true to the heart of our
message is still that of joyous freedom.

The theological facet of this position is decisive, yet I leave it
unformulated just now. A programmatic or administrative facet
I may, however, attempt to formulate, in a way that will for some
be maybe more provocative than the theological, and perhaps

more immediately illustrative. And as we shall see, theology will be implicit.

The suggestion is this. Opportunity for a Buber-like participation of Christians, deliberate, self-conscious, constructive, in the life and thought of other communities can begin to be planned— in consultation and collaboration with those with whose destiny the participant is involved. I mean that the selection, the training, and the activity of Christian participants in the process of specifically Islamic history can, and I think will, be done by Muslims and Christians sitting together and discussing it constructively, and implementing it jointly, and so on in each case. I do not know whether mission boards and mission secretaries are yet ready to call and pay for a planning conference on Christian missions to India to which an equal number of Hindus and of Christians will be invited. I seriously suggest that it could be not only significant but fruitful, and not only fruitful but right. I do not know whether the missionary movement will move in this collaborative direction. I see participation as an actual burgeoning development, from which the older concept of "missionary" may (through inertia or choice) diverge, and perhaps presently peter out.

I am thinking here not in terms simply of social welfare work (although in the planned-parenthood movement there is an incredibly profound as well as important realm for activist-cum-theoretical collaboration), or of any evading of crucial theological and centrally religious issues. To imagine so is to underestimate the seriousness and authenticity of men of other forms of faith, who after all are at least as concerned with the central and ultimate issues as are we. A conference such as I suggest would be fruitful, and would not be dull.

Of course, such a co-operative conference would have to be called not as a gesture, but genuinely, and because one had deeply seen that what God wants accomplished by Christians in India tomorrow can be discovered in no other way. We can begin to participate helpfully only when we recognize that we have first much to learn.

The thesis that the Hindu process in India does not contain within itself (that is, its traditional self) the answers to modern India's questions (I mean, the answers that God wishes given), which is the thesis on which Christian missions have rested, must be counterbalanced with a recognition that the Christian process does not contain within itself those answers to modern India's questions either, even religious questions (and again I mean the answers that God wishes given). Our theologians have not yet seen and formulated this, but those who have practical experience with India will doubtless recognize at least its practical truth.

In the conference idea, as I have said, new theological ideas are implicit. It was in part the mission field that spurred the theologians into ecumenical awakening. Conceivably it is in part from the mission field also that those pressures will arise, and those insights and delights, that will help the theologians towards a more serious awareness of what the modern world is really like.

The fundamental prerequisites for a participant, apart from grace and faith (I leave them undefined) are: from the Christian side, humility and love; and towards the religious tradition of those among whom he finds himself, a profound respect and the ability to perceive God redemptively at work through that tradition. Being an academic, I am tempted to stress also that he should have a good deal of knowledge about that tradition; yet this is less important at the start than the respect and the perception. Without these and the openness and sensitivity that they imply, the missionary movement must be called off. With them, its day has just begun.

We have mentioned the Ramakrishna and other missionaries now serving in Christendom. Lest our own perceptions of what a missionary is should make that idea rather frightening, let me refer also to such illuminating and helpful writings as a critique of Christian ethics by a careful and serious Muslim, published by a Western university press, and to a report of a commentary on the Gospel of St. John by a Hindu, a commentary reverent, perceptive, novel. No true appreciation of Christian participation in other developments is available except to those who *as Christians* can see others' participation in our Christian development as something not only to be understood but to be welcomed, and not only to be welcomed but to be sought. If this seems too radical, let me recall that haunting injunction (I hold my Christian loyalties seriously) that we must do unto others only what we would that they do also unto us. We are not accustomed to taking this seriously at an interfaith level, but we have to learn. We have no right to send missionaries to any group from whom we are not ready to invite missionaries.

The old concept of missions was unilateral. I propose a new concept of mission that is multilateral.

V

We come, then, to my final point. At this stage of the argument I would like to conclude by generalizing the participation theme. I suggest that a profoundly new phase has begun in the religious history of mankind, a phase on which the whole world today seems to be embarked. Not merely is it one in which one man or group may participate in the religious evolution of another tradition. We are reaching a further point where eventually each will participate in all. The new emergence is the unitary religious history of mankind.

One may not like the word "religious" here, and it may not survive. It is hardly likely that the term "spiritual" will be more widely appealing; maybe we should call it simply the humane history of mankind. A number of observers of the local scene in the West have been greatly impressed by the convergence between the Christian and the secular. I am more impressed by the coming convergence (I do not say fusion) of the Christian and the Hindu and the Buddhist and the Muslim. This convergence is actually happening, in ways whose depth and intricacy and novelty are beyond comprehension. We may be frightened by it, or bewildered, or exhilarated; in any case we must try to understand it.

We said earlier that on inquiry a static notion of an "Islamic religion" gives way, once one looks more closely, to a dynamic notion of Islamic history, to the Islamic process in history in which Muslims have been participating. Now we may add that the notion even of Islamic religious history gives way to the truer concept of an Islamic strand in the religious history of mankind. Given the hostility among communities, ranging from open warfare on the battlefield to intellectual and emotional boundaries of stupendous rigidity, I am not unaware of the boldness of such a concept. Yet I press it, as that towards which we are inescapably moving, for each person, certainly each group.

This is already happening in college classrooms and in some churches, in the sense that for good or ill the religious life of an individual is beginning to be thought and lived in the light of the religious heritage of all the world. It began to happen some while ago in the sense already mentioned, that what Westerners do and think constitutes for good or ill a consequential force in the religious life of Asia. Something approximating it has been happening all along in China and Japan, where Westerners have never understood how a man can "belong to two or three religions at the same time," as they ineptly phrased it, but where the situation can more truly be conceptualized by saying that Chinese and Japanese have participated in a process constituted by more than one tradition. Once one thinks of it, it turns out that we in the West have long participated, each of us, in a complex process constituted by the Christian and the Greco-Roman-humanist traditions in elaborate interaction; most Western Christians would feel grievously out of place in an Ethiopian Christian church, for example, representing the Christian evolution in a process less adulterated by the other Western factors.

I do not mean that Christians will cease to be Christian, or Muslims Muslim. What I mean is that Christians will participate, as Christians, in the religious history of mankind; Muslims will participate in it as Muslims; Hindus as Hindus; Buddhists as Buddhists. I am a Presbyterian, and will never shake off my delightful Calvinistic Puritanism until the day I die; yet the community in which I participate is not the Presbyterian, but the Christian. I participate as a deliberate though modified Puritan in the Christian community, and the Christian process. In much the same way, I choose to participate as a Christian in the world process of religious convergence.

One of the things that I have learned from my Christian heritage is that part of Christian truth, by which I mean part of the ultimate truth of the universe, is that all mankind is ultimately one community. It is my delight to find that this is part of the Islamic truth also, and of Hindu truth, and of Buddhist. One of the tasks open to us today, and beckoning to us, is to *participate* in God's creative process of bringing into actual reality what has until now been an ideal reality only, that of a world-wide human community. The missionary assignment for the next phase of human history is to take the leadership in this participation: to help realize the vision that we can begin to see, wherein we all participate in each other's processes of moving towards God. Not that I have forgotten that the initiative is His: each separate tradition is the process of response to God's initiative, and the current phase is our response to His bringing of the religious communities of the world into mutual involvement. To responsible missionary leaders, among others, is offered the task of guiding that response.

All human history is *Heilsgeschichte*. Not the history of Israel only, the old or the new, but the history of every religious community. This has always been true, but we are the first generations of Christians to see this seriously and corporately, and to be able to respond to the vision. We are the first generation of Christians to discern God's mission to mankind in the Buddhist movement, in the Hindu, in the Islamic, as well as in the Jewish and the Christian. Having discerned it, let us not fail to respond to it.

8

Comparative Religion: Whither—and Why?*

Smith's audience in this essay is not Christian missionaries or Christian theologians, as such. It is, nonetheless, very definitely a Western academic audience which until quite recently had had few qualms about calling primitive, ancient, and Asian traditions "non-Christian." The audience is the professional scholarly community in the comparative study of religion, or, in European terminology that has come into wide use, the history of religions.

The agenda for discussion is the general subject of methodology for the history-of-religions field: By what formal procedures can the efforts of scholarship on the subject of man's religions be conducted, tested, and validated? It is no small question. The laborers in this academic vineyard are far from agreement, for example, on criteria by which an investigator could be said to have "understood" a religious tradition in which he does not participate. On the one hand, what real datum is there to religion without the experience that only a participant can have? On the other, what integrity is there to description without the autonomy, even the detachment, of the observer? To achieve

---

* Reprinted in abridged form from Mircea Eliade and Joseph M. Kitagawa, eds., *The History of Religions: Essays in Methodology* (Chicago: The University of Chicago Press, 1959), pp. 31–58. Copyright by University of Chicago Press. Used by permission.

"understanding," how many parts of empathy must we mix with how many parts of analysis? The recipe is far from settled, and there is hardly a cook in the comparative-religion kitchen who does not contribute to this broth.

That Smith's contribution to the discussion opts for a dialogue of the observer with the participant will be a familiar point to many readers, for this essay is one of Smith's more widely read and often discussed writings. It appeared (with a substantial apparatus of notes not included here) in a Chicago volume of essays on methodology in the history of religions which has remained in print for over fifteen years—years during which Smith has repeatedly voiced an impatience with methodological discussions and an unwillingness to place himself out on any particular methodological limb; from time to time since 1965 he has indicated a preference to be what I have called a "methodological pluralist." Yet if Smith has specified no one method for gathering data (at a 1974 Iowa conference on methodology he indicated that he would hardly enjoin the scanning of book titles for occurrences of the word "religion" as a requirement for anyone else), still he has specified a very definite test for validating results: that a description of religion be mutually affirmable by participant and observer.

*As far as our empathy/analysis contrast is concerned, Smith manifestly seeks the best of both worlds, saying that both aspects of understanding should be present—at different "levels." The matter is subtle, and the discussion continues in the scholarly literature. And as long as this article continues to be taken seriously, the case for mutuality as a principle of academic discourse about religion, especially of course about living traditions, will have strong support.—*ED.*

The thirteen-volume *Encyclopaedia of Religion and Ethics* (ed. James Hastings, 1908–21, and re-issued) is an impressive work. Not only does it serve as a great warehouse of information, indispensable to all careful students of the world's religious history. More than that, it may be taken also as a symbol. I see it as typifying a culmination of the first great stage of scholarship in this field: the accumulation, organization, and analysis of facts. This stage began, one may say, with the Age of Discovery, when Western Christendom reached out to the rest of the world, probing, exploring, gradually becoming aware of peoples and places far beyond its erstwhile horizon. There were brought back accounts, weird or wonderful, of other men's religions—at first haphazardly, as travelers' tales, later in more ordered fashion and more abundantly. The nineteenth century saw the rise of a great attempt to give this matter serious and disciplined consideration: searching out material, recording it carefully, scrutinizing it systematically, interpreting it. This was the task of the universities, which gradually enshrined Oriental studies and anthropological studies and here and there established chairs of *Religionswissenschaft*, the study of religion.

In our day a new development in these studies is to be discerned, inaugurating a second major stage, of rather different type. In suggesting this, I do not mean that the first phase is finished. It continues, and will continue. Information of increasing breadth and increasing precision, analyses of increasing complexity, presentations of increasing erudition and subtlety, must and will go on. I would hold, however, that these things, while not superseded, are being now transcended. The exciting new frontiers of inquiry and of challenge lie at a new and higher level.

In the first phase there was amassed an imposing knowledge about other peoples' religions. In the second phase it is those other peoples themselves that are present. The large-scale compilation of data of the nineteenth century and up to the First World War has in the twentieth century and particularly since the Second World War been supplemented by a living encounter —a large-scale face-to-face meeting among persons of diverse faith.

In a sense, the modern counterpart to the *Encyclopaedia* are such facts as that in 1936 Sir Sarvepalli Radhakrishnan was appointed Spalding Professor of Eastern Thought at Oxford; in

1952 the Institute of Islamic Studies was opened at McGill with half its teaching staff and half its students Muslims; from the 1950's visiting Buddhist scholars have been invited to the Chicago Divinity School; and so on. Westerners professionally concerned with the Orient, including its religious life, are now expected to visit the communities about which they write, and most do keep in frequent and close personal touch. And just as in medicine a graduate may not practice until he has added an internship to his academic training, so at McGill University it is a formal requirement for the doctorate in Islamic Studies that the candidate "at some stage in his adult life, before, during, or after his work at McGill shall have spent some time (preferably at least two years, and in any case not less than the equivalent of one academic session) in the Islamic world." It is coming to be recognized that part of the cost of setting up a department of Oriental studies in a Western university is the provision of travel funds and arrangements for what is unfortunately still called "leave," for the staff, who must have access to the Orient just as much as a chemistry professor must have access to a chemistry laboratory.

Moreover, it is not only the professional students that are affected; the general reading or thinking public has also moved into the new phase. When the *Encyclopaedia* was published, intellectuals of Europe, and America had available in it and in a series of books information about the "non-Christian" world; today intellectuals and also others find that they personally have Buddhist or Muslim neighbours or colleagues or rivals.

Future historians, it has been said, will look back upon the twentieth century not primarily for its scientific achievements but as the century of the coming together of peoples, when all mankind for the first time became one community.

The new world situation is compelling us to explore what I might call the essentially human quality of our subject matter. If we can effectively come to grips with this, we shall have taken a very considerable step forward towards doing justice to the study that we have ventured to take on. But it is not easy. The implications are many and subtle. Religion being what it is, and man being what he is, the task of adequately conceptualizing the personalization that is today involved will demand our best efforts, of careful scholarship and creative thinking.

The present essay is an exploratory attempt to delineate and to analyse trends and to urge desiderata.

The argument may be summarized briefly, in pronominal terms. The traditional form of Western scholarship in the study of other men's religion was that of an impersonal presentation of an "it." The first great innovation in recent times has been the personalization of the faiths observed, so that one finds a discussion of a "they." Presently the observer becomes personally involved, so that the situation is one of a "we" talking about a "they." The next step is a dialogue, where "we" talk to "you." If there is listening and mutuality, this may become that "we" talk *with* "you." The culmination of this progress is when "we all" are talking *with* each other about "us."

I

The first and altogether fundamental step has been the gradual recognition of what was always true in principle, but was not always grasped: that the study of a religion is the study of persons. Of all branches of human inquiry, hardly any deals with an area so personal as this. Faith is a quality of men's lives. "All religions are new religions, every morning. For religions do not exist up in the sky somewhere, elaborated, finished, and static; they exist in men's hearts."[1]

We are studying, then, something not directly observable. Let us be quite clear about this, and bold. Personally, I believe this to be true finally of all work in the humanities, and believe that we should not be plaintive about it or try somehow to circumvent it. It is our glory that we study not things but qualities of personal living. This may make our work more difficult than that of the scientists but it makes it also more important, and in a significant sense more true. Ideas, ideals, loyalties, passions, aspirations cannot be directly observed, but their role in human history is not the less consequential, nor their study less significant or valid. Nor do the transcendent matters to which these may, no doubt inadequately, refer, but a status in the universe the less solid. A galaxy may be larger, but a value I hold to be not only more important but at least equally real and in some ways more real.

A fundamental error of the social sciences, and a fundamental lapse even of some humanists, has been to take the observable manifestations of some human concern as if they were the concern itself. The proper study of mankind is by inference.

The externals of religion—symbols, institutions, doctrines, practices—can be examined separately; and this is largely what in fact was happening until quite recently, perhaps particularly in European scholarship. But these things are not in themselves religion, which lies, rather, in the area of what these mean to those that are involved. The student is making effective progress when he recognizes that he has to do not with religious systems basically but with religious persons; or at least, with something interior to persons.

Certainly there has been and remains a great deal of preliminary work to be done in the realm of tangible data, of what I have called the externals of religion. It is only as these are accurately established, that the study of the religions themselves can proceed; and this latter must continually be revised as the former become more exactly known. It is not a crucial question whether the same scholars do both tasks or whether there is division of labour. Nor is it worth quarreling about the relative value of the two; both are needed. What one would advocate is clarity. The time has come when those in this field must recognize to what extent an article or a book or a conference or a committee is concerned with the externals of the history of the religion and to what extent with the history of the religions themselves. I am also suggesting that over the past century there has been, and am guessing that in the near future there will

increasingly be, a development in the direction of more awareness that religions are human involvements.

The point may be illustrated. When in 1934 John Clark
Archer published a general textbook, *Faiths Men Live By*, the
title was arresting. Nineteenth-century scholarship did not think
in such terms, though today the attitude is almost standard.
Personalization can be achieved also, however, in the case of the
religion of an historical community that has ceased to exist:
Henri Frankfort's *Ancient Egyptian Religion* (1948) differs from
the first Western monograph on the subject, by Adolf Erman
(1905), in considerable part as a study of people over against a
study of data—or, more precisely, the study of a people's religious life over against a study of their gods, their doctrines, their
institutions, and the like. The difference is in attitude and treatment. Erman's study fails not because it deals with the externals
(they are important, and he was an important Egyptologist) but
because it makes the mistake of presenting these as the religion
itself. Our plea would be that from now on any study of exter-
nalia recognize itself as such; that only those deserve to be accepted as studies of religion that do justice to the fact that they
deal with the life of men.

Part of the personalization of our studies is evinced in the shift
over past decades to a primary interest in the major living religions of the world. (The phrase "living religions," which has
become current, is itself significant.) Whereas at the turn of the
century a typical introductory course in this field would emphasize "primitive religions," and a typical book would address itself
to "the nature and origin of religion" (the phrase implicitly
postulates that the reality or truth of religion is to be found most
purely or most surely in its earliest and simplest forms), today it
is normal to give chief or even sole attention to Hindus, Buddhists, and Muslims, along with Christians and Jews—groups
that among them constitute the vast majority of today's population, and among them claim most forcefully to represent religion's highest and truest development. And whereas once such
attention as was given to the great religions was primarily to

their scriptures and historically to their early, classical phases, today these religions are seen primarily as the faith of present-day groups.

In the case of the living religions this matter affects not only the conception of what is being studied, but also the method employed. First, there is an important epistemological point. In the study of a religion other than one's own, a knowledge of its institutions, formulations, and overt history may be derived from things. But if they are seen as clues to a personal quality of men's lives, then a sympathetic appreciation of this quality may at least in part be derived from having adherents of that faith as informants and perhaps even as friends. Of the various ways of finding out what something means to the person concerned, one way is to ask him.

Moreover, books by Western scholars about, say, Buddhism are increasingly being read by Buddhists. Few Western authors have been conscious of the wide extent to which this has become true. Even fewer have grasped its important implications. I would put forward two propositions, both rather bold and perhaps more in process of becoming cogent than actually valid as yet but, I am persuaded increasingly important. The first is that it is no longer legitimate to write in this field for any but a world audience. Many think that they are addressing books and articles to one particular community (normally their own), but these are in fact read by others, and especially by that other community that they are about. Muslim writing about the West or about Christianity or Christendom, though in Arabic or Urdu or whatever and produced for Muslim consumption, is being studied and analyzed by Western scholars, and the results published. This has two sets of consequences: a somewhat sensitive awareness of the fact is beginning to be not without its effect on the course of Muslim writing itself, in addition to the effect on Western orientation to Islam.

It is much more widely true that books by Western scholars expounding, let us say, Islam to Westerners, or analysing the rise of Mahayana Buddhism in terms of an academic tradition of secular rationalism, are increasingly studied by those concerned. So far this fact has led to only limited awareness and had very limited effect on the course of such Western writing, but these have begun to be discernible and must increase. The effect on the East has been great, and is growing. Western writing on Eastern religion has had, in the course of the last hundred years, because of its substance, an influence on the development of those religions themselves that certainly deserves careful historical investigation; on the whole, because of the form in which it has mostly been cast, it has in addition been causing resentment and is beginning to elicit protest. Certainly anyone for whom comparative religion studies are something that might or should serve to promote mutual understanding and good relations between religious communities cannot but be concerned at this contrary effect. Even by those to whom this is a moral point not essentially germane to the intellectual principles involved, it may yet be recognized that a situation has arisen wherein anyone who writes about a religion other than his own today does so, in effect, in the presence of those about whom he is speaking.

If nothing more, an author not alert to the point that we have been urging: namely, that a religion is a personal thing in the lives of men, is today being alerted to it by the increasingly live reaction to his writing of those men themselves.

As it becomes more widely recognized that the comparative religionist speaks in the hearing of those he describes, this will inescapably have its effect at least on how things are put and perhaps also on the kind of thing said. The point is that an author must write not only more courteously but more responsibly.

I would contend that not only is such a development taking place but that it ought to take place, deliberately and rapidly. For I would proffer this as my second proposition: that no statement about a religion is valid unless it can be acknowledged by that religion's believers. I know that this is revolutionary, and I know that it will not be readily conceded; but I believe it to be profoundly true and important. By "religion" here I mean as previously indicated the faith in men's hearts. On the external data about religion, of course, an outsider can by diligent scholarship discover things that an insider does not know and may not be willing to accept. But about the meaning that the system has for those of faith, an outsider cannot in the nature of the case go beyond the believer; for their piety *is* the faith, and if they cannot recognize his portrayal, then it is not their faith that he is portraying. There are complications regarding historical change; I recognize that a religion develops, whereas few believers do recognize this, so that what once was true about it may no longer be so, and the insider can speak authoritatively only for the present. There are other complications too. But on the fundamental point I have no qualms: I would hold emphatically that fruitful study must recognize this principle. Indeed, it is not really a limitation but a creative principle; for it provides experimental control that can lead a student dynamically towards the truth.

Non-Christians might write an authoritative history of the Church but however clever, erudite, or wise, they can never refute Christians on what the Christian faith is. The only way that outsiders can ever ascertain what Christianity is, is by inference from Christian work or art or deed; and they can never be better qualified than those Christians to judge whether their inferences are valid. Indeed, some Christians have maintained that in principle no one can understand Christianity who does not accept it. I do not go so far, but I recognize substance in this contention. I recognize also that a similar point applies to all religions. Anything that I say about Islam as a living faith is valid only insofar as Muslims can say "Amen" to it.

The reverse is certainly not true. Not every statement about Islam that is acceptable to Muslims is *ipso facto* true: one can flatter or beguile. Nor need outsiders simply follow Muslims: it is possible both in theory and in practice for an outside scholar to break new ground in stating the meaning of a faith in, say, modern terms more successfully than a believer. At the present time [1959—ED.], for instance, Muslims themselves have not been able to give an intellectual statement of their faith that succeeds well in communicating meaning to a Western audience. The task of a non-Muslim scholar writing about Islam is that of constructing an exposition that will do justice to the Western academic tradition, by growing directly out of the objective evidence and by being rationally coherent both within itself and with all other knowledge, and at the same time will do justice to the faith in men's hearts by commanding their assent once it is formulated. It is a creative task and a challenging one.

Whether or not this particular argument carries full conviction, we pass on. The general point that has been made is that in the new conditions of the modern world the comparative study of religion has moved into a new phase—first, in that the object of inquiry has on a quite new scale been seen to be communities of persons. Enough has been said to emphasize the point that the implications of this development are far from negligible.

II

Our second point is that the subject of inquiry also has been taking on a personalized quality: the investigator. Formerly the scholar was seen, ideally, as the detached academic intellect, surveying its material impersonally, almost majestically, and reporting on it objectively. Such a concept is characteristic of the academic tradition of Western Europe; one might be bold enough to add, characteristic particularly of nineteenth-century Western Europe. One cannot belittle that tradition or its accomplishments, in our field or in others. Yet in three ways the situation has become more complex since.

First, the detachment was felt in this particular case to mean, *inter alia*, that the scholar studied religion but did not (at least, *qua* scholar) participate in it. Most of the significant academic advances in the study of religion before the First World War or thereabouts were made by the secular rationalist. In mid-twentieth century, on the other hand, he is joined, if not superseded, by the explicit Christian as a student of non-Christian religions, or at least by the serious searcher as a student of all religions, in the West. Seventy-five years ago it was widely held in universities that a necessary qualification for an "impartial" or scientific study of religion, including the religions of other communities, was that the student be without a faith of his own, be not *engagé*; at the present time, the contrary view is not unfamiliar.

Secondly, the Western scholar in this as in other fields is being joined by investigators from other civilizations—where the secular-religious dichotomy of the West does not, or does not so fully, obtain. In the Muslim world, India, the Buddhist countries, writers in this field will largely write, one may expect, as Muslims, as Hindus, or as Buddhists. This much at least may be conceded, that along with the academic tradition of detached secular study of religion, there is growing in both Christendom and elsewhere a religiously related scholarship of religious diversity. To some extent in the future these studies, it would seem, are to be carried out by religious people for religious people.

The third aspect of this development is that even the secular rationalist is coming to be seen as a person like another: not a god, not a superior impersonal intellect, monarch of all it surveys, but a man with a particular point of view. Secular rationalism may be the right road, may be the Truth as it claims to be; but it has come to be felt that there is no *a priori* intellectual or universal reason for supposing so from the start, so that it may sit in unchallenged judgment on equally massive and venerated traditions, Christian, Hindu, or whatever, that make the same claim. The decline of Western Europe's world position, the rise of existentialist philosophies and moods, the Western "return to religion," the rise of Communism, and the resurgence of Eastern civilizations on a religious base, have all conspired to bring about this new situation, wherein the secular intellectual, like the religious believer, takes his place as a member of one group of men, one of the world's communities, looking out upon the others.

Each writer in this field is beginning to be recognized and to recognize himself as the exponent or champion of one tradition in a world of other persons expounding or championing others.

III

The next step follows rather closely. When both the writer and that about which he writes become personal, so does the relationship between them. As we have said, the present position is an encounter. When persons or human communities meet, there arises a need to communicate. What had been a description is therefore in process of becoming a dialogue.

To talk about people is not the same as to talk to them; nor is this quite the same as to talk with them. The need for these last two steps in comparative religion is beginning to be felt, only gradually perhaps in universities but urgently by the churches. The word "dialogue" has actually been coming much to the fore in recent years, with both the Roman Catholic Church and the Protestant. Major movements are afoot. It is perhaps too early yet to say whether this is the form into which the earlier unilateral preaching of the evangelistic missionary movement is being transformed; there seem to be forces working in that direction, not the least being the vitality of the faiths addressed. Might it not be that the next step in missions would necessarily be one where one religious group says to another, "This is what we have seen of the truth, this is what God has done for us; tell us what you have seen, what God has done for you; and let us discuss it together"? Provided that this is sincere, it seems entirely legitimate; though if a participant privately hoped or believed that out of a genuine discussion the other side would come to a preference for his side, then it may still be evangelical.

To situations of these kinds the comparative religionist may respond in various ways, though to me it hardly seems reasonable that he not respond at all. First, he may participate in the dialogue, as a member of one or other group. In a meeting between, let us say, Christians and Buddhists, it is clear that the conversation would proceed the better if the latter contingent included a well-qualified Buddhist student of comparative religion. One would hardly organize a dialogue with Hindus without inviting Radhakrishnan. Indeed, in a sense all members of the encounter are in effect expected *ipso facto* to end up as in some sort comparative religionists; presumably some of them might well start so. In the Christian case specifically (and to some extent the same would apply in theory to the Muslims, though in practice today it would clearly not) it would be felt by some that the comparative religionist would be out of place as a protagonist in any encounter. Such a feeling has been due to two things: the Western tradition of academic non-involvement, on which we have already commented, and the Christian tradition of exclusivism and proselytism. I would argue that these last two are not (or will become not) obligatory elements of the Christian faith, and indeed my personal view would be that the very value and even the purpose of Christian dialogue with other faiths may well be a Christian learning at last to apprehend one's own faith fully and loyally (and perhaps more truly?) and simultaneously to appreciate the quality and even the ultimate validity (in the eyes of God) of others'. Many today say that this is in principle not possible. I venture to believe that it is and that dialogue may be an avenue of the Church's reaching it.

The second role that the representative of our studies may play in the encounter between faiths is that of chairman. Some of us may aspire to qualify—indeed to regard this qualification as almost the essence of our work. One objective of training might be formulated as equipping the student with such an understanding of at least two religions, and of the problems of relationship, that he can serve as a mediator or interpreter between them, or at least as a kind of broker helping them to interpret themselves to each other.

In fact, in one or other of these roles not only might the scholar of comparative religion seem professionally involved; perhaps the department of comparative religion may become institutionally so. It is perhaps not unlikely that over the next, say, twenty-five years, departments of comparative religion in various parts of the world will formally become places where such dialogues deliberately and explicitly take place, formalizing and systematizing the intellectual encounter between representatives of diverse traditions. In North America such a process has already begun at McGill, Chicago, and Harvard. The move will be effectively launched only when there are counterparts in Asia.

The third role is that of observer. If the comparative religionist chooses not to participate in or to moderate the dialogues that are in fact increasingly taking place, at least he can hardly fail to take a (professional) interest in what is going on. It is part of the contemporary history of the religions (and conceivably one of the most profound matters in the whole history of religion) that they are encountering each other, both on systematized occasion and informally in the coffee houses of the world.

The scholar is presented with the task of conceptualizing the dynamic processes at work. My earlier contention was that a statement about a religion, in order to be valid, must be intelligible and acceptable to those within. In order to be sincere, and of any use, it must also of course be intelligible and acceptable to the outsider who makes it. This can be generalized so that herein is posed one of the fundamental tasks of our studies today. I would formulate it thus: *it is the business of comparative religion to construct statements about religion that are intelligible within at least two traditions simultaneously.* This is not easy, it has not been done systematically in the past and almost not done at all; but it is intellectually important and historically urgent.

Since the scholar presumably works from a university, that is, within the academic tradition, the statement that he produces must first of all be meaningful and cogent within that tradition. That is, it must satisfy his own trained and inquiring mind, and must satisfy all the most rigorous standards of scholarship. In the particular case where the encounter is between the academic tradition of the West and a particular religion, the statement that is evolved must satisfy each of two traditions independently and transcend them both by satisfying both simultaneously. In the case of an encounter between two religious groups, let us say for example Christianity and Islam, the scholar's creativity must rise to the point where his work is cogent within three traditions simultaneously: the academic, the Christian, and the Muslim. This is not easy, but I am persuaded that both in principle and in practice it can be done.

This kind of constructive thinking is necessary in order to provide the intellectual basis for the meetings between communities that are today taking place. Like other intellectual advance instigated by actual problems of evolving human conditions, however, it has worth in itself, and implications far outreaching the immediate issues. In principle, the drive is towards the construction of an intellectual statement (or history) of the diverse religions of mankind that ideally does justice to all of them as well as standing independently, a statement that will be cogent to a reasonable man who is a member of any faith or of none. This leads us on to our fourth major consideration, where the personalization of our studies with which we began eventuates in their attaining fully human status, overcoming the local or particularist. In this lies the culmination of this development of our work, and to it we now turn.

IV

The emergence of dialogue is important not only in itself but for its further implications. Once it is achieved, its significance transcends the achievement, opening the way to a still newer stage. For a dialogue may lead (in some individual cases has led already) to reconciliation, to an enlarged sense of community. In any case, and at the least, it implies articulateness on two sides. This is incipient, and major. No longer is the prosecution of these studies exclusively a Western prerogative. Japanese are studying Eskimo animism and Christianity, Muslims are diagnosing Western secularism, the theorizing of Hindus about comparative religion is becoming widely known. Muslims, Hindus, and Buddhists are learning to talk to Christian and Western scholars, as well as being talked to, and in the process are studying religious diversity itself. Thus the Western scholar is slowly coming to have not only an Asian (or African) informant as his source, an Asian critic as his audience, an Asian scholar as his teacher, but, perhaps most significantly of all, an Asian colleague as his collaborator.

Certainly we are only at its beginning, but the long-term trend promises to be towards a transformed situation, where an international body of scholars writes for a world audience. This essentially new and potentially highly significant emergence brings to light what I see as the culmination of the contemporary transformation. As with the other stages, it makes vivid what was always in principle true but hardly grasped.

I have argued that one cannot study religion from above, only from alongside or from within—only as a member of some group. Today the group of which the student recognizes himself as a member is capable of becoming, even is in process of becoming, world-wide—and interfaith. This is the significant matter.

For once the community becomes large enough, and if consciousness keeps pace, that process is fulfilled whereby the study is no longer an objective inquiry carried on from the outside, but a human study carried on from within. Even a face-to-face dialogue gives way to a side-by-side conversation, where scholars of different faiths no longer confront each other but collaborate in jointly confronting the universe, and consider together the problems in which all of them are involved.

For finally it will be recognized that in comparative religion man is studying himself. The fact of religious diversity is a human problem, common to us all. It is becoming an incorporated, internal part of the fact of being a Christian that other intelligent, devout, and righteous men are Muslims, Hindus, Buddhists. Even the non-religious man is engaged in living in a world where his fellows are of unreconciled faiths. Every man is personally involved in all man's diversity. Man here is studying one of the most profound, one of the most perplexing, one of the potentially most explosive aspects of his own modern situation. We all are studying the fact that our human community is divided within itself religiously.

The practitioner of comparative religion, then, I am suggesting, may become no longer an observer vis-à-vis the history of the diverse religions of distant or even close communities, but rather, a participant—in the multiform religious history of the only community there is, humanity. *Comparative religion may become the disciplined self-consciousness of man's variegated and developing religious life.*

We may look now for a history not so much of the disparate religions but of man's religiousness. Such a history should be persuasive to students of that total history, themselves from diverse faiths. It should be such and they should be such that they can recognize and acknowledge their own separate communities within it, and at the same time recognize and acknowledge the totality, of which also they are learning to be part. Such a history should in particular trace and clarify—even explain- -the rise, at a certain period of human history, of the great religions as separate entities. Perhaps also sheerly by being written it would give some intellectualization to the fact that again, in the present period of human history, those great religions seem in some degree to be in process of ceasing to be quite so separate, even perhaps of ceasing to be quite so surely entities.

The student of comparative religion begins with the postulate that it is possible to understand a religion other than one's own. In our day, this postulate is being tested—urgently, severely, by our concrete human situation. We are called upon to make good our claim, in practice, and quickly. To meet this challenge demands that we rethink our purposes, recast our basic concepts. But there is also the promise that if we do meet it, the results may contribute to that largest of contemporary problems, the turning of our nascent world society into a world community.

A religious history of man has yet to be written, concerning itself with the development of us all rather than primarily with the development of each. It is interesting to note, however, that titles are beginning to be phrased as "the religions of *man*" and the like. Presently may there be a symposium in which scholars from different faiths will write chapters not each on his own faith but perhaps each on other aspects of the total development, in a way agreeable to all?

V

It would, of course, be an over-simplification to hold that an over-all development such as has been here outlined has gone forward quite straightforwardly and steadily. I do suggest, however, that it is in fact possible to characterize any study of a religion other than one's own, or of interrelationships, as falling under one or other of these headings. I suggest also that there has been on the whole a gradual movement in the direction indicated. I contend further that clarity here will prove of major benefit. We must become conscious, and self-conscious, on this matter. Students would do well to ask themselves, concerning any account or any project that they meet, in which category it falls: impersonal/it, impersonal/they, we/they, we/you, we-both, or we-all. A writer should clarify in his own mind which kind of book or article he is proposing to write; and an organizer, which kind of university department, of conference, of journal, he is proposing to run.

Though the various principles that we have adumbrated are beginning to be recognized, the performance, one must confess, is as yet sadly inadequate. It will be a good while yet before anything is achieved on the level of interreligious communication and dialogue, let alone on that of multireligious consciousness, that can be compared for quality to the impressive monologue of the *Encyclopaedia.* When a work does appear worthy of typifying achievement in this realm, we predict that it will be written by a person who has seen and felt, and is morally, spiritually, and intellectually capable of giving expression to, the fact that we—all of us—live together in a world in which not they, not you, but *some of us* are Muslims, some are Hindus, some are Jews, some are Christians. If he is really great, he will perhaps be able to add, some of us are Communists, some inquirers.

If the great religions are true, or even if any one of them is, then such a work is possible; and if it is written, it will be essentially true. For have we not been told that men are brothers, that in the eyes of God (or, one might equally say, of reason) the human community is the only real community there is? And that the two matters of supreme importance are the relations among persons within that total community, and the relations between men and God?

Notes

1. The quotation is from my earlier essay, "The Comparative Study of Religion: Reflections on the Possibility and Purpose of a Religious Science," *McGill University, Faculty of Divinity, Inaugural Lectures* (Montreal, 1950), p. 51.

9

Objectivity and the Humane Sciences: A New Proposal*

This essay marks an end to our collection, but not a conclusion to it. There is a simple reason for this: that the diverse themes opened up in Smith's essays published over a sixteen-year period do not all proceed in one direction or toward one goal, and no one selection would sum them all up. I would reject for an image of this state of affairs the impression that many Westerners first have of Asian music, namely, that one ends without building to a conclusion. Rather, the more useful metaphor for our collection should be that of a net still in the process of being woven, where strands continuing in different directions extend onward in interaction with each other.

This final selection, concerned with values in scholarly and intellectual life, is once again a selection that would seem not to focus on religion. But Smith's views in this area are related to his treatment of religion in a network of ways, of which we might mention only a few.

First, religion as subject-matter (particularly the diversity of religious expressions and traditions) is a useful test case to see

* Reprinted in abridged form from the *Transactions of the Royal Society of Canada* (Ottawa, Royal Society of Canada, 1975), pp. 81–102. Copyright © 1975 by Wilfred Cantwell Smith. Used by permission.

whether one's academic methods and approach are fair to the data. Smith indicates that the West has, in the instance of India, often failed, through a focus on externals, to describe that land's religious heritage adequately.

Now, for Smith, what is at fault here is the justification of such externalism in the name of the emphasis on objectivity found in Western science and philosophy. Objectivity is objectionable in a twofold sense: when people are treated as objects, not only human community is threatened, but proper intellectual understanding. Such interpretations, however factually correct they may seem, should be abandoned as morally wrong because they disrupt community; but moreover, they are for Smith conceptually wrong because they fail to take adequate account of persons.

Second, religion is a pattern of commitment to truth, and the quest for truth in the Western intellectual heritage is closely akin to religion. As in the case of religious communities, academic dedication to truth and learning should know no internal professional boundaries. "The disciplines," meaning the circles of professional academics engaged in different fields of study, make Smith uneasy. Since an inclusive academic community is inherently valuable (both morally and as conducive intellectually to truth), any fragmentation of it through the use of jargon, and through emphasis on discrete methodologies as over against a unifying subject matter, constitutes a threat reminiscent of the Tower of Babel. Smith prefers a style of generally intelligible academic exposition which he takes to be in the British university tradition, over against the closed circles of "disciplines," which he sees as an infection of modern academic life perhaps derived from the German universities. "Interdisciplinary" efforts, then, amount merely to making the best of what was a bad thing to begin with.

There is a close parallel between Smith's test of interreligious discourse in the previous essay and Smith's criteria for valid description of man: namely, that the participant should be able to recognize himself in, and mutually affirm, the description offered by the observer. Smith sees the ideal of objectivity to have been wrongly borrowed from the natural sciences by the behaviorists. To be objective is impersonal; Smith's preference is the opposite, which he calls "personalism."

In the 1960's Smith had made common cause with the social sciences, finding congenial their emphasis on the study of contemporary groups. In the early 1970's, however, sometimes to the dismay of the interdisciplinary-minded even among his close associates, he became sharply critical of the social sciences—holding their methodological objectivity to be anti-social and, he would say, anti-truth.

Smith's audience for a fuller version of this essay, on June 4, 1974, was the meeting in Toronto of the Royal Society of Canada, the country's most distinguished and prestigious academic society, to which members are elected from the various disciplines of the arts and sciences. At its best, perhaps, that society could point toward the kind of inclusive community of inquiry, the kind of mutuality of intellectual concern, which is Smith's ideal.—ED.

The idea that I shall set forth in this essay is a relatively simple idea; yet I am aware that it is radical, and ramifying. It is advanced here in the conviction, however, that the time has come for a major new departure, a new vision. Given the depth of our contemporary crisis, both in our civilization and in the university, that the idea is in some ways drastic seems not necessarily a weakness.

By the phrase "humane sciences" in the title of this essay I mean all study of man by man. The current fashion has been to pattern the university's intellectual activity into three or four realms: the natural sciences, plus perhaps the life sciences; the social sciences; and the humanities. I am concerned particularly with the division between the last two, which has indeed become more than a fashion, with its practical institutionalization as well as its deep theoretical involvements. The phrasing "humane sciences" may suggest a superseding of that dichotomizing within the study of human affairs, as well as a continuity between our study of the external world of things and our study of ourselves.

My phrase "humane sciences" is not simply a translation from the French. It discriminates, instead, between human knowing and humane knowing. All science is human science. The natural sciences are human sciences, in the sense of human activities, human products: they constitute knowledge and study on the part of man. In contrast, it is our knowledge *of man* that I am calling humane knowledge—that is, knowledge of man by man.

I personally am a humanist, in more than one sense of the word; not incidentally but committedly, not passively but as an active champion of humanist values as indispensable to the whole university as an institution, and indispensable to all knowing as a human activity. At Harvard, I discovered myself formally categorized within a social-sciences division. Certainly I hold it manifest that to understand humanity is to understand man as social. I hold it manifest also that an understanding of human society does not deserve to be called scientific unless it is ruthlessly rigorous, critical, rational. We have hardly yet attained humane sciences in these senses; hence our fragmentation. It is in the hopes of contributing towards such attainment that I make bold to proffer my suggestion.

I

I wish—dare I admit it?— to move beyond the goal of objectivity. I am conscious that it will at first blush seem offensive to many to find that sacred symbol of scientific and rational thought being irreverently considered and critically scrutinized—and assessed as rationally inadequate in this field. Yet I am inviting you, not to a simple rejection of it, but to go beyond it. If you are kind enough to hear me out, I am hopeful that my argument may emerge as constructive, and even helpful; as rational, and even scientific—as well as humane.

It is frequently recognized that pure objectivity is, alas, difficult or even impossible to attain. But it often seems to be assumed that perfect objectivity would be a good thing if only we could be innocent enough or clever enough to achieve it. I disagree. I would postulate a law: that what man does is misunderstood if conceived wholly from the outside. You may be quick to retort that modern knowledge makes us more aware than ever also of the contrary law: that what a man does is misunderstood if viewed wholly from the inside. Of course! Subjectivity is no royal road to truth, either. Of much that goes into our actions, our feelings, our moral choices, our thinking, we are ignorant; and of what we know, much we distort. We deceive ourselves, as well as others. We elude ourselves, not only outsiders. Objectivity, the externalist approach, was developed to get beyond the inadequacies of individual interiority. That it, too, in its turn is proving inadequate, untrue, less than rational, means that we must go, not back to subjectivity, but forward to a larger vision.

It has been held that objectivity is not merely characteristic of, but foundational for, scientific knowledge. I would submit that objectivity is the correct, scientific way of dealing intellectually with objects, but that it must be supplemented when what is to be known is other than, or more than, an object—for instance, is a person, or a work of art, or a tribe. I contend that it is pseudo-scientific, is scientific in only an imitative and not a genuine sense, to apply to the study of human affairs the objectivity that is appropriate for the study of other fields. To claim that a procedure or a conceptual pattern is scientific, one must do more than demonstrate that it has been fruitful in a quite different area of study.

In the second place, the alternative to the objective has been thought to be the subjective. I submit that in addition to the subjective, my individual and internalist awareness of something or someone, or of myself, and to the objective, the impersonal, externalist knowledge, there is a third position which subsumes both of these and goes beyond them; and that it is this that we should posit as our goal, in the humane field, the study of man by man. I call it critical corporate self-consciousness.

A third characterization of objectivity is that an observer's knowledge of a given object is in principle available also and equally to any other observer—ideally, to all mankind. By corporate self-consciousness I intend knowledge that is in principle available both to the subject him- or herself, and to all external observers; or in the case of group activities, to both outside observers and to participants. Again, this means in principle all mankind. We shall be returning later to the distortion of knowledge involved because the ideal of objective knowledge is confined to outsiders, this being a limitation in principle.

The transition from consciousness to self-consciousness was one of the profound, crucial moments in human evolution. Its first appearance represents the emergence of man. The transition from consciousness to critical consciousness was another extraordinary moment, marking the appearance and expansion of science. The emergence of critical self-consciousness is the major transition through which the human race is perhaps now about to go. Man's awareness about himself and his neighbour will expand to become truly scientific, truly rational, not when man's knowledge of man is objective, which is theoretically inapt and practically disruptive, but rather, when human self-consciousness becomes fully critical and fully corporate, ideally embracing us all.

By corporate critical self-consciousness I mean that critical, rational, inductive self-consciousness by which a community of persons, constituted at a minimum by two persons, the one being studied and the one studying, but ideally by the whole human race, is aware of any given particular human condition or action as a condition or action of itself as a community, yet of one part but not of the whole of itself; and is aware of it as it is experienced and understood simultaneously both subjectively (personally, existentially) and objectively (externally, critically, analytically; as one used to say, scientifically).

Introduced here is a decisive new principle of verification. The intellectual pursuit in humane studies of corporate self-consciousness, critical, rational, empirical, is scientific in various senses—including that of its alone being subject, in the deepest sense, to a valid verification procedure. In objective knowledge, that a first observer's understanding has done justice to what is observed is testable by the experience of a second and third observer. In corporate critical self-consciousness, that justice has been done to the matter being studied is testable further by the experience of the subject or subjects. Often the test of another observer is in principle not available; since unlike what obtains in the world of matter, human situations are not precisely repeatable. In any case, it is inadequate, partly because all observers are inherently less than the whole of mankind (a point to which we will return), and partly because it is intrinsic to human experience that that experience appears differently, and in fact *is* different, from the inside and from without. No statement involving persons is valid, I propose, unless its validity can be verified both by the persons involved and by critical observers not involved.

In a sentence, then, my proposal is that all humane knowledge (that is, all knowledge of man by man) is in principle a form of self-consciousness. We have, historically, reached a point where we can, and, I suggest, must, recognize this, and choose it. The proper goal of humane knowing, then—the ideal to which we should aspire academically, scientifically—is not objectivity but corporate critical self-consciousness. My submission is that this will yield truer knowledge, opening up enormously rich rewards of understanding, and, importantly, of valid verification.

II

In this presentation I can develop the positive proposal, obviously a major matter, only slightly. Much of my argument here will be critical, rather: that, as an ideal in this field, objectivity is wrong, in that it fails to give true knowledge in human affairs.

My argument rests both on theoretical considerations and on empirical observations. At the theoretical level, of rational analysis, the basic premises of my thesis are two. The first is that man is patently different, in ways highly significant, from material objects, and from all other forms of life known to us; so that any ideas from man that underestimate his uniqueness or downplay his humanity are *prima facie* inadequate, or worse. Human qualities such as self-transcendence, a sense of justice, a creative and destructive imagination, a capacity to respond to and to create beauty, a capacity for wickedness and also for dignity, freedom, compassion, rationality; a cunning capacity to decieve and also a drive or aspiration towards intellectual and moral integrity; the pursuit of truth; a sense of remorse, an ability to forgive; moral responsibility; and so on and on and on: these are manifest facts; and frankly, it strikes me as rather stupid either to propound or to put up with theories that, whether in their presuppositions or in their conclusions, or often both, fail to do justice to these facts.

The second theoretical premise is the equally inescapable one that the knowing mind is human; is not outside, and cannot get outside, the human race to look at it externally, objectively. This has long been recognized as a difficulty, in objectivist theories; but it has been regarded also as a regrettable weakness, and attempts have been made to reduce its significance as far as possible, to approach as closely as feasible to externalized viewing. I, on the other hand, regard the participation of the knowing mind in the humanity that it seeks to know as an asset, and not merely an inescapable fact; and I would order our intellectual inquiry in accord with it, not in opposition to it nor in flight from it. My reason is simple: that it helps us to know.

The empirical observations on which my position rests have had to do primarily with cross-cultural inquiry, specifically the Western academic study of the Orient and more especially of its religious history. The position that I am propounding is, I maintain, of quite general relevance; its validity, however, has been rendered primarily conspicuous in both the successes and the failures evident in the endeavour of one civilization to understand another. The limitations and indeed the fallacies of both the subjective and the objective types of knowledge have here become clear, as has also the enormously rich potential of the new transcultural critical self-consciousness.

Let me illustrate.

In Western understanding of, let us say, India there has been a clear advance through successive stages: first, ignorance; secondly, impressionistic awareness of random parts of the culture (an outside subjective stage); thirdly, a growingly systematic and accurate yet insensitive and externalist knowledge of facts (an objective stage); and more recently, and richly promising, the beginnings of serious and even profound humane understanding of the role and meaning of those facts in the lives and the culture of the persons involved. (This last carries strikingly forward, in some cases almost transforms, India's own self-awareness, the erstwhile insider's subjective knowledge.)

I call this last stage personalist. I hope that it is hardly necessary to insist that by "personal" I do not mean "individual." Personality is profoundly social. The opposite of individual is social; the opposite of personal is impersonal. The earlier stage was of an impersonal knowledge of facts (it aimed at impersonal knowledge). The newer stage is of a personal knowledge, and understanding, of the meaning of those facts, in the cultural life of Indians. It generates statements about Indian life that both Indians and outside observers can jointly recognize as true, and illuminating.

Let us look at a particular item within the religio-cultural complex which Westerners objectified by giving it the name "Hinduism." Recently I had occasion to visit the South Indian city of Madurai, site of a famous and magnificent temple. Western awareness of this temple has gone through successive stages: from ignorance, through impressionistic travelers' tales of its sumptuousness and grandeur, and then through a meticulous and detailed knowledge of the temple as an object of observation (it has, for instance, among other glories a hall of several hundred pillars, on any one of which a descriptive analysis of the intricate art work could constitute a Ph.D. dissertation topic). I had never been that far south in India before, and I was entranced to observe the temple, in which I spent many hours. An interesting question, however, is what one looks at when visiting a sacred structure. More engaging than the temple itself were persons worshiping within it, and their worship. Or we may say, the important matter was the living complex constituted by the temple and the worshipers within it.

The truth of the temple manifestly lay not in the building itself as an object but in its significance for, and interaction with, these men and women. The temple primarily is what it is perceived by them as being; or at the least, their perception of it is incontrovertibly part of its truth. Recent Western understanding of the temple has gone forward dramatically as scholars have come to recognize that the role of such a temple in the consciousness and the lives of persons is part of what one must know if one sets out to know the facts. It is out of Hindu religious consciousness that the temple arose in the first place, and in that consciousness that its reality primarily continues to lie

Actually, in this particular case there never was a time when Westerners' apprehension of the building was merely and totally objective; since if it had been so, they would not even have recognized it as a temple. The most rank outsider always participated in Hindu consciousness to at least *that* extent. The notion of temple, and that of symbol in general, are humane concepts, not objective. No building is objectively a temple. No space is objectively sacred. No object is objectively a symbol, in and of itself: an object becomes a symbol in the consciousness of certain persons. That a given object symbolizes one thing for one group of people, something else for another group, and perhaps nothing at all for a third group, is a fact without which human history would have been dramatically different from what it has been and is. Merely objective knowledge of what serves some people symbolically has in historical fact distorted outsiders' observations in the realm of religion. It not merely fails to illuminate religious conflict, but actually has often contributed to it. The only knowledge that is adequate of the history of religion, and indeed of culture, and indeed of human history generally, is a knowledge that participates in the consciousness of those involved.

To understand a symbol, I am contending, one must both

know it objectively and in addition must know what it means, has meant, in the lives and consciousness (including the subconsciousness) of persons. This varies, of course, from community to community, and from age to age. It is never quite precise: like a poem, only much more so, it shimmers with a whole range of meanings, and of innuendos—overt, subtle, and hidden, conscious and unconscious, quiescent or activating. Moreover, it is not simply what the symbol itself means to persons, but what life means, what the universe means, in the light of that symbol. My studies have led me to the view that a symbol in principle never means exactly the same thing to any two persons (nor even necessarily to any one person at different times), although on this both Carl Jung and Mircea Eliade, two of the greatest twentieth-century scholars in this realm, have tended to presume otherwise, without, I feel, having thought the matter through. We need not go into that issue here, beyond my indicating that as an historian I am inescapably aware of diversity and change. In any case there is no dispute that the meaning of things in human history lies in their relation to persons, in the interaction of human beings with them, and not in themselves as objects.

An objective knowledge of the moon, provided by natural science, is different from, and for humane studies is less than, a knowledge of the role of the moon in human life and in the history of human culture and poetry and religion and love, and even in the history of human science and technology and space travel. The natural sciences cannot tell us about the moon all that we want to know, or that is worth knowing. Let us not be so fatuous as to forget this massive fact.

I would go further, and insist that the role of the moon, or of the temple of the moon in ancient Babylon, or of that temple of Minakshi in Madurai—their significance in the consciousness and the lives of men and women—is not fully nor even accurately knowable by behavioural sciences either, which are externalistic and explicitly leave out of consideration the self-consciousness of those involved. To understand man, and to understand history, it is necessary to know not only what man does, the behaviourist's little province, but what he refrains from doing; what he dreams of doing, what he fears to do; what he does with exultation, hesitation, guilt, or boredom. An action is not understood unless one discerns what courage went into it, what routine, what integrity or duplicity, what choice. To read a statement in a Sanskrit or an Arabic text one must know what it says but also what it takes for granted. One must listen to what people leave unsaid, be sensitive to their failures, recognize what they do in terms of what they are trying to do. As Wilhelm Dilthey long ago insisted, the behaviour of human beings is to be seen and interpreted as within a context of the consciousness that gives meaning to their lives, and to that behaviour.

To return to that Madurai temple. I remarked earlier that from the very beginning outside observers went beyond mere objectivity to knowing that it was indeed a temple. Their notion of what a temple is, however, was limited and inadequate, in some cases distorted. Some Christians, some secularists, had a quite imperceptive or false sense of Hindu religious life, even though they were not unaware that it existed and was important. It is worth noting that even now, despite a great deal of progress in this realm, so that our understanding of temples in general and of this one in particular is vastly richer, deeper, truer, than was theirs, nonetheless it is still the case today that no one on earth, neither Hindu nor outsider, yet fully knows what a temple is. No one fully understands what it means, in human life and in cosmic life, that that building is "a temple" for those persons. Our knowledge of templeness, if I may coin a term, is much better than it was; yet it is by no means complete.

To appreciate the significance of that temple as a temple, we must get inside the consciousness of those for whom it is a sacred space, must know how it feels and what it means to be a worshiper within it; although we must also know all the objective facts about it; and as well, in order to know the full truth about that temple, we must know its significance in the lives of shopkeepers in its environment, must know its crucial role in the whole city life and the town plan of Madurai, and must know how it is perceived also by the small iconoclastic Muslim group in the area, for whom temple worship is a sin, and how it is perceived by atheists, and by Marxists, whose analysis of its economic role is impertinent in one sense but not in both.

True knowledge of the temple as a human institution, as a reality in the life of several million persons, must incorporate its role in the consciousness of worshipers within it as well as of critical observers on the outside, insofar as each is valid. The insider, if he is dedicated to full knowledge, full self-consciousness, must and ideally will incorporate into his awareness the truth that outsiders see, so far as it be true; and the external observer, if he is resolute to attain to true knowledge, must incorporate into his understanding not only his critical analyses from the outside, in all their rigour, but also the reality that the temple constitutes in the life of the pious devotee, which after all is the primary reality of the temple as a fact in human affairs. There is no theoretical reason why these two persons and indeed why all human beings whatever who may direct their attention to this temple, should not ideally converge in synthesizing all this truth into one conceptual apprehension. This would then constitute what I am calling corporate critical self-consciousness, with all of us recognizing in full awareness that some of us worship in this temple and some of us look on. This, and not the outsiders' partial knowledge, is, I am suggesting, the ideal at which to aim for human knowledge of that particular reality.

When at the beginning of last century the Christian missionary Bishop Reginald Heber, who had almost no understanding of Hindu spirituality, said that "The heathen in his blindness/ Bows down to wood and stone," he was objectively right, but, I would argue, scientifically wrong.[1] At least, he was humanely wrong. For he failed to participate in the consciousness of those whom he was observing, or to realize that that consciousness was part of the truth of what he was looking at. They bowed down not to the sticks and stones, but before what these symbolized to them. In his externalist observation, Heber was a forerunner of modern behavioural scientists. Like them, although in one sense what he said was true though misleading, in a much more significant sense he just did not know what he was talking about.

Any objectivist, externalist, behaviourist observer who leaves out human consciousness simply does not know what he is talking about. This applies equally to my former colleague at Harvard, B. F. Skinner, and to that early missionary.

For these matters may be generalized, throughout the comparative study of the history of religion, through the whole range of comparative culture, and finally, I am suggesting, to the entire humane field. The truth of anything that pertains to man lies, and has always lain, not merely in that thing, but in man's involvement with it; and in the end, in man's involvement through it, with himself, with his neighbour, and with God—or with the universe *in toto*.

To understand the faith of Buddhists, one must look not at something called "Buddhism." Rather, one must look at the world, so far as possible through Buddhist eyes. In order to do that, one must first know the data of the Buddhist tradition, at any given moment observable, concrete, objective. It can, and therefore must, be studied objectively with the utmost rigour of scholarly exactitude: meticulous care, scrupulous precision, and erudite attention to minutiae.

This inescapable first step is, however, only the first step: he who takes it is an historian of a religious tradition, not yet an historian of religion. The faith of a Buddhist does not lie in the data of the Buddhist tradition. The locus of faith is persons. We have understood the tradition intellectually, academically, truly, only insofar as we can see human lives in terms of it: can see the significance that the data had for men and women, and the meaning that life had for them because of those data. Such significance—not only in their overt behaviour but in their aspirations, fears, imagination, embarrassment, self-understanding—is not an object, and cannot be known objectively.

Yet it can be known, more or less accurately. To apprehend it requires interpretation, imagination, insight, perceptivity, human sympathy, humility, and a whole series of qualities—

human qualities. It requires, fundamentally, that the student be himself a human person, and indeed as fully human as may be. Not flashes of imagination, necessarily: it may demand long hours, or years, of patient, careful wrestling with the material. And not "subjective" interpretation, by any means: requisite are careful discipline, cross-checking, the framing of hypotheses and the testing of them against new data or against personal inquiry, and a whole apparatus of critical and self-critical procedures. To be an historian is an art; and, like most arts, it requires skill.

To understand any human behaviour, any human feeling, any human hope or vision, is to recognize that if you had been in that situation, you would have had that particular act or quality or value-judgment as one of your options. Not that you would necessarily have acted as another did; that would deny human freedom, and indeed one has not understood *him* unless one recognizes that he might not have acted that way either, although in the end he in fact chose to do so. But to act so would strike you as one of the reasonable possibilities. The goal of the historian or other student of human affairs is to reconstruct a given situation in the past or at a distance from oneself with such accuracy that we can know what that situation, factually, was; and with such insight that we can know how it felt to be a human being in that situation. To be an historian of religion is to aim at discovering objectively the cumulative tradition of Jews, Hindus, Buddhists, Muslims, and the rest as each actually developed, and at appreciating what it must have been like to be a Jew, or a Hindu or whatever, at a particular point in history.

To be an historian, or indeed a rational student in any humane field, is to stand imaginatively in the shoes of other men. This is possible, in principle, because we are persons, and because they are persons. Two of the fundamental qualities of humanity are the capacity to understand one another and to be understood.

Not fully, certainly. Yet not negligibly, certainly.

Human beings are that kind of reality, it so happens, that any given two of them—no matter how close together, no matter how

far apart, in space, time, culture, temperament—any two of them
can arrive at an understanding that is neither one hundred per
cent nor zero. There is no person on earth that I can fully understand. There is and has been no person on earth that I cannot
understand at all.

III

I would turn now to a related aspect of the problem: that
objectivity inherently disrupts community, both in principle and
in practice. Ideally, humane knowledge in my sense postulates
community, and serves to promote it. My assertion that all
knowledge of man by man is *ipso facto* self-consciousness is true
insofar as all mankind is one. It becomes operative *pari passu* as
that unity is seen, is felt, is willed. Otherwise, as has been the case
in the recent past, some men may seek external, objective knowledge of other men. Such external knowledge not only emerges
out of separateness, however, but corroborates and furthers it.

One aspect of this is the issue of experimentation. A sub-facet
of this that has struck me increasingly of late is the deception
practiced on persons being studied. A second major issue is that
of manipulation, control. Objective knowledge is inherently
oriented towards the alienation of persons from each other.

Even at a less gruesome level, there is the issue of prediction. A
criterion of objective knowledge, sometimes set forth also as a
goal, is the ability to predict. This derives from the natural sciences, and once again illustrates that objective knowledge is
appropriate in our dealings with objects. There are certain ways,
too complicated to go into here, and with important caveats
anyway, in which statistical prediction about groups of people is
a function of certain kinds of knowledge. Otherwise, however,
the notion of predicting personal behaviour—and I mean, as
ever, the predicting by some persons of the behaviour of other
persons—though less horrendous than experimenting with them
or manipulating them, is still both irrational and inhumane. It is
both, in that it denies human freedom. It is an intellectual error,

since it postulates what is in fact not true, that men and women act mechanically, or quasi-mechanically. It affronts human dignity, since it therein ignores or dismisses one of man's most precious, and most characteristic, qualities.

Objectivity began as a reaching out towards universalism. What was objectively true was, in principle and by aspiration, to be true for all men, explicitly as contrasted with the subjective impressions of private parties. This worked quite well in the natural sciences: that is, for our knowledge of a world that is equally external to all of us. It breaks down, however, when what is involved is a knowledge of some men by other men. The fallacy, though significant, was somewhat less apparent with intra-cultural studies. In general, within one's own civilization, whatever the theory, the knowers, the "experts," have been participants to some more or less saving degree in the human institution or activity that they studied, or at least have had some more or less surreptitious understanding of it, some more or less effective sympathy with it, and even some sense that their work is relevant to its members. In cross-cultural studies, on the other hand, and conspicuously sometimes in the studies of alien faith, the objectivity and externality of the knowing have meant quite definitely that the knowledge was designed for, and relevant to, non-participants in the phenomenon, the society, the institution, being analysed.

The academic work of Western scholars in Asia has regularly been clearly and explicitly designed to be read by, and to be of interest to, the closed group of one's "discipline" back home. One can argue, citing some scandalous examples, that this is immoral; but this is not the occasion for that. I have argued that such work does not render a knowledge that penetrates to the personal level of those studied, which is the most significant level.

The third argument, however, and the important one here, is that objective knowledge is idiosyncratic. Just as the early Christian missionary wrote for Christians "back home," so the sociologist writes for sociologists—and this, not as a foible, like his jargon, but on principle. I suggest that there is an intellectual flaw here: one might dub it the "we/they" fallacy. The thing is amusingly sectarian: one writes only for those who share certain presuppositions (and whose ritual is certain methodologies).

The fallacy is enshrined in the contemporary concept of "discipline," which postulates a particular body of people who esoterically share a certain body of knowledge. It has come to be the case that academics of the objectivist, as distinct from humane, sort read professionally only within their own discipline, write only for members of their discipline, and accept as authoritative criticsm the judgment only of what they call their peers. This is subjectivity with a vengeance! Group subjectivity, no doubt, but subjectivity for all that. Objective knowledge of man leads to subjective knowledge by man. The importance of this has been little understood, but is major. Its contribution to fragmentation is serious.

Clark Kerr of California formally proclaimed an acquiescence in this multifarious subjectivism when he coined the term "multiversity." That repellent notion is a modern paraphrase of Heraclitus's *idia phronesis*, "idiosyncratic understanding," which the university was developed in order to transcend. The concept of diverse disciplines is a sophisticated and institutionalized version almost of the collapse of the university idea, a failure of rational knowledge. So deeply have most of us become victims of it, however, that criticism of it is hardly either understood or entertained.

The social and human devastation wrought by this disciplinary development has been tragic (almost in the Greek sense: there is a certain nobility in the failure). Human loyalties have therein tended to be transferred from the college or university where one works, to the "professional society" of one's discipline, of which one is a member (with consequent segregation, if not alienation, within the institution, of scholars, from both students and colleagues). The university, with this orientation, tends to be no longer a community of scholars: neither among disciplines, nor between teachers and students. A concept of "career" has been constructed, with the result that academic rewards are then conceived in terms of outward status rather than increased vision. The training of graduate students into the closed circle has taken precedence over the educating of undergraduates. And so it goes. Despite these social and human ramifications, however, which are woeful, it is the intellectual fallacy involved that concerns me here primarily: the notion that knowledge of man (of ourselves, after all) is the domain of a multitude of disparate idiosyncrasies.

Recent "interdisciplinary" efforts are an attempt to construct a ladder by which to climb out of a hole into which genuinely humane studies never fall. One hopes that they are promising. One fears, however, that at best they but enlarge the group of those who know externally (perhaps ideally to include the whole behavioural-science community), without transcending the subjectivity endemic to a closed group of outside observers.

IV

About this linking of objectivity with the fragmentation of community, however unorthodox the idea, I am very serious. Yet I leave it now to move on to my final section, on the role of the knower in humane knowledge. Objectivity drastically fails to do justice not only to the known but to the knower, not only to the object of knowledge but to the subject. There is an under-appreciation of man as learner; objectivity inherently misapprehends what happens or should happen to the student or scholar in the process of inquiry.

The notion of objectivity has grown out of work in the natural sciences, where the external world one investigates is seen as less than man, as in some fashion beneath him, where what is known seems legitimately to be subordinated conceptually to the mind that knows. In objective knowledge there has arisen a stress on method, suggesting that what is known is dominated. (I recently heard an academic professional in the field of English literature say in the modern fashion that that field constitutes a body of material to be mastered. One might better think in terms of the student's being mastered by it, surely!)

Learning in the humanities involves being open to what may be greater than oneself—greater, at least, than one has been until now. The process of knowing is a process of becoming. It is not a matter of using means, but of assimilating ends. Not *primarily* a matter of using means, certainly: of applying certain methods external to oneself. The point of learning about the natural world is the joy of knowing, and/or the resultant ability to change that world. The point of learning about man is the joy of knowing, which inherently comprises a changing of oneself.

Methods, so far as they are systematized in formal methodologies, not only are, but are calculated to be, separable from the person who employs them. The concept of methodology, and the stress on method in education, imply that one knows ahead of time what one wants, and has only to find out how to get it. In principle it is possible to learn techniques without ceasing to be basically the kind of person that one was before, to come out of the learning process at heart as one went into it. If a university teaches only techniques, proffers only methods of ascertaining what one already wishes to know, then of course students should decide what they wish to know, and in effect should employ the experts to satisfy these aspirations. They should *use* the university for their own purposes.

Such an enterprise runs counter to humane knowing, which is an exercise in the meeting between persons, even across the centuries or across the world. Humane learning is an exploration of what man as such (or shall we not, rather, say, "we human beings") has been, may be, and truly, ultimately is. It is therefore not technical, not subordinable to methodological rules. In personal relations the use of technical procedures, unless rigorously subordinated to primarily personal considerations, is not merely inappropriate but potentially disruptive. Man cannot know man except in mutuality: in respect, trust, and equality, if not ultimately love. In this realm of knowing, accordingly, the attitude with which one approaches one's data proves to be at least as significant, as consequential, as the methods with which one handles them. One must be ready not only to receive the other man, but to give oneself. In humane knowledge, at stake is one's own humanity, as well as another person's, or another community's. And at issue is humanity itself.

We have come full circle, then, to my basic thesis: that the new mode for humane knowledge is in terms of a disciplined corporate self-consciousness; critical, comprehensive, global. To study man is to study oneself—even when one man, or one society, studies another separated by much space, or time, or both. It is to expose one's actual self to one's potential self, and, through knowing something new, to become a new kind of person.

In principle, then, for all mankind to know each other is for all mankind to become one community. And vice versa: only as we move towards community can we come to know. Our solidarity precedes our particularity, and is part of our self-transcendence. The truth of all of us is part of the truth of each of us.

Several years ago I had occasion to characterize the study of comparative religion as moving from talk of an "it" to talk of a "they," which became a "we" talking of a "they," presently a "we" talking of "you," then "we" talking "with" you, and finally —the goal—a "we all" talking together about "us." The study of comparative religion is the process, now begun, where we human beings learn, through critical analysis, empirical inquiry, and collaborative discourse, to conceptualize a world in which some of us are Christians, some of us are Muslims, some of us are Hindus, some of us are Jews, some of us are skeptics, some of us are inquirers; and where all of us are, and recognize each other as being, rational men.

One of the most deeply significant facts about any person is, whom he means when he says "we." In principle, I am contending, the academic intellectual cannot rest content until he means "we human beings," across the globe and across the centuries; and his work must be seen, by him and others, as a contribution towards that. As a beginning, and as a concrete practical step, he must move towards meaning not "we in my discipline" but "we persons involved in this particular study": those of us being studied, and those of us studying (in a discipline, if you like, though I should prefer to say, in a university). The truth then that we seek is a truth that can be recognized, assimilated, existentially and critically validated, by both sets of us within this new community.

Some may feel that I have gone too far, or have been too strident, in my urging our superseding the objectivist orientation. I have come to feel strongly on the matter through awareness of the pain and resentment on the part of Asians before the aggression of much Western academic scholarship. More recently and nearer home, I have become alert to the growing resentment of students in Western society before modern academic study's aggression against the person.

The established doctrine and the to some seemingly ritualized procedure of the current phase of the modern scientific movement seem massively solid, not easily opened to critical revision. As an historian of religion, I am familiar with the difficulty, intellectual and emotional, that the carriers of a system have when their orthodoxy is challenged, the basic postulates of their tradition questioned. If some of you, as carriers of scientific orthodoxy, resist my heresy, if you find bizarre my thesis that there is something starkly and profoundly awry with the impersonalism of modern orientations to knowledge, at least you must find sobering the practical, and by implication also theoretical, challenge posed by student dissidence. Universities that have succumbed to the recent mis-orientation, as I call it, are subject to that otherwise enigmatic wonder, of appearing repellent to the sensitive. I hope that no one underestimates the deep significance of the alienation from the university of many of our most intelligent, sensitive youth.

And indeed this matters outside the university too, in Western society at large. As our culture has become increasingly permeated with what passes for a scientific outlook on knowledge and the world, and also on human matters, the increasing success in dealing with things has been accompanied, as everyone knows, with an increasing sickness of personal and social life: the depersonalization of social procedures, the fragmentation of community, the alienation of the person from his neighbour, from himself, and from the world. As a humanist, I resist blaming this on science; I blame it on objectivization, mis-applied from natural science to thinking about human affairs. And I certainly resist the notion that the only alternative to objectivity is subjectivism —a fallacy so loudly proclaimed that some believe it and in fleeing from depersonalizing objectivity turn to irrationality, at times through the use of drugs.

Impersonalism is in human affairs, I argue, bad science, is irrational; and the alternative to both objectivity, which is false, and subjectivity, which is radically inadequate, is a rational personalism in community.

I have insisted on the deep differences between our knowledge of the material world and our knowledge of ourselves. Yet I believe in the unity of knowledge, as I believe in the unity of mankind. I think it perhaps not absurd to suggest that the concept of corporate human self-consciousness could subsume, in the end, the natural and the life sciences without infringing their integrity. The human enterprise of science, man's study of the objective world, may be envisaged as a corporate critical consciousness on the part of mankind of the material world in which we live as it appears objectively to us men, and not detachedly as absolute knowledge of that world as it is in and of itself. Given the ecological crisis, the atomic bomb, and the moral implications of modern genetics, to understand all science responsibly as ideally a form of critical human consciousness seems not perhaps unreasonable.

However that may be, we must learn to see our knowledge of ourselves in this light—lest we invite both error and disaster.

NOTES

1. In the well-known hymn "From Greenland's Icy Mountains," stanza 2 (1809).

For Further Reading

There is always something more to be read. Ask a student writing an essay whether he has all the material he'd like, and the answer will probably be negative. Ask a professor for a single reading suggestion, and you may well receive a book list several pages long.

To follow up the network of Smith's concerns in this collection, likewise, may entail a multiplicity of readings for any individual topic. For readers wishing to pursue Smith's views further, a virtually complete bibliography of his books and articles through 1975 is offered. Nonetheless, a few suggestions may be useful by way of introduction, as a reader's guide to the Smith corpus.

For the beginner the simplest, and possibly the most engaging, discussion of the details of specific religious traditions is offered in The Faith of Other Men *(1962), which originated as a series of radio talks. To document his view that religion is best thought of not as an entity but as an outlook on the world, Smith illustrates each major tradition by sketching how one of its central features is meaningful in the life of a participant.*

Another simple introduction, not to the spirit of specific traditions but to an appreciation of man's religiousness in general, is provided in Smith's three-page essay "Religion as Symbolism" in the new edition of the Encyclopaedia Britannica *(1974). Writing in the "Propaedia" volume of general introductions to different fields of learning, Smith proposes that not only visual symbols and ritual patterns, but conceptual symbolization such as the notion of "God" amount to ways of expressing a view of the world and of life in it.*

We turn now to more technical suggestions for readers interested in pursuing aspects of Smith's views beyond what the collection in this anthology has furnished. I use a three-part grouping here and in the full bibliography which follows: (a) religion generally, (b) education, area studies, and social concern generally, and (c) Islamic subjects.

On religion in general, Smith's substantial book is The Meaning and End of Religion *(1963). As we have indicated, it combines a history of the concept "religion" based on word usage, with a view of religion as a blend of personal faith and cumulative tradition, and with a plea that the usages "a religion" and "religions" referring to the externals of tradition be dropped. Another principal line of Smith's thought is his notion of truth, readably discussed through illustrative examples in* Questions of Religious Truth *(1967). It is given an important, more technical, treatment in "A Human View of Truth" (1971), which appears in the context of discussion with philosophers of religion and with a response by Smith in Hick, ed.,* Truth and Dialogue *(1974). Two current theological topics of the mid- and late 1960's to which Smith addressed himself are featured in "Religious Atheism" (1966) and "Secularity and the History of Religion" (1969).*

Two recommendations in the area of education, both bearing on how we conceive of academic fields and how Western divisions of subject-matter may prove inappropriate for Asia, are "The Islamic Near East: Intellectual Role of Librarianship" (1965) and "Non-Western Studies: The Religious Approach" (1965).

Though Smith's specific work on Islam has not been the focus of this anthology, the reader should not overlook Islam in Modern History *(1957); Smith's most widely read work, it draws on the ideas of historical process and conscious choice which we have explored. Also characteristic of Smith's work is the analysis of not only institutions but ideas as having developed historically: the Islamic notion of law now traditional is not quite as old as one might have thought, according to "The Concept of Shari'a among Some Mutakallimun" (1965), and the Islamic germ of Smith's historical analysis of the noun "religion" may be seen in "The Historical Development in Islam of the Concept of Islam as an Historical Development" (1962). More on the West's emerging conceptualization of Asian traditions is "The Comparative Study of Religion in General and the Study of Islam as a Religion in Particular" (1962). An institutional development which Smith traces is the emergence of the Sikhs as a distinct religious group, in "The Crystallization of Religious Communities in Mughul India" (1969).*

We end with a beginning. Readers who have a biographical interest may wish to take Smith's McGill inaugural, "The Comparative Study of Religion" (1950), not as an isolated opus but as an overture stating several themes of Smith's later opera. —*E.D.*

PUBLICATIONS OF WILFRED CANTWELL SMITH THROUGH 1975

Books

Modern Islām in India: A Social Analysis. Lahore, Minerva, 1943.
Revised edition: London, V. Gollancz, "1946" (sc. 1947).
Reissued: Lahore, Sh. M. Ashraf, 1963, 1969; New York, Russell & Russell, 1972; and pirated edition, Lahore, Ripon, 1947.

Pakistan as an Islamic State. Lahore, Sh. M. Ashraf, "1951" (sc. 1954).

Islam in Modern History. Princeton, Princeton University Press, 1957.
Reissued: London, Oxford University Press, 1958; New York, New American Library (Mentor Books), 1959; London, New English Library (Mentor Books), 1965.
Taped for Recording for the Blind, Inc., Washington, 1973.
Translated into: Arabic (pirated, 1960; authorized, 1975), Swedish (1961), French (1962), Indonesian (1962–64), German (1963), and Japanese (1974). Portions translated into: Urdu (1958–59, 1960) and Arabic (1960).

The Faith of Other Men. Toronto, Canadian Broadcasting Corporation, 1962.
Enlarged edition: New York, New American Library, 1963.
Reissued: New York, New American Library (Mentor Books), 1965; London, New English Library (Mentor Books), 1965; New York, Harper & Row (Torchbook), 1972.
Translated into: Swedish (1965).

The Meaning and End of Religion: A New Approach to the Religious Traditions of Mankind. New York, Macmillan, 1963.
Reissued: New York, New American Library (Mentor Books), 1964; London, New English Library (Mentor Books), 1965.

Modernisation of a Traditional Society. Bombay, Calcutta, etc., Asia
    Publishing House, 1965.
Questions of Religious Truth. New York, Charles Scribner's Sons; and
    London, V. Gollancz Ltd., 1967.
    Translated into: Japanese (1971).

ARTICLES ON RELIGION GENERALLY

"The Comparative Study of Religion: Reflections on the Possibility and
    Purpose of a Religious Science." In: *McGill University, Faculty of
    Divinity, Inaugural Lectures* (Montreal, McGill University, 1950),
    pp. 39–60.
"The Christian and the Religions of Asia." In: *Changing Asia: Report
    of the Twenty-Eighth Annual Couchiching Conference: A Joint
    Project of the Canadian Institute on Public Affairs and the Canad-
    ian Broadcasting Corporation* (Toronto, Canadian Institute on
    Public Affairs, 1959), pp. 9–16.
    Reprinted: *Occasional Papers*, Department of Missionary Studies,
    International Missionary Council (World Council of Churches),
    London, no. 5 (April, 1960); also as "Christianity's Third Great
    Challenge," *The Christian Century* 77:17 (April 27, 1960) 505–
    508; also, abridged, *The Beacon*, London, 39 (1962) 337–340.
"Comparative Religion: Whither—and Why?" In: Mircea Eliade and
    Joseph M. Kitagawa, eds., *The History of Religions: Essays in
    Methodology* (Chicago, The University of Chicago Press, 1959), pp.
    31–58.
    Translated into: Urdu (1962), Japanese (1962), and German (1963).
"Some Similarities and Differences between Christianity and Islam: An
    Essay in Comparative Religion." In: James Kritzeck and R. Bayly
    Winder, eds., *The World of Islam: Studies in Honour of Philip K.
    Hitti* (London, Macmillan; and New York, St. Martin's Press, 1959),
    pp. 47–59.
    Translated into: Urdu (1964).
"Mankind's Religiously Divided History Approaches Self-Conscious-
    ness," *Harvard Divinity Bulletin* 29:1 (1964) 1–17.
    Translated into: German (1967).
"Secularism: The Problem Posed," *Seminar*, New Delhi, 67 (1965) 10–12.
"Religious Atheism? Early Buddhist and Recent American," *Milla wa-
    Milla*, Melbourne, 6 (1966) 5–30.
    Reprinted: John Bowman, ed., *Comparative Religion: The Charles*

Strong Trust Lectures 1961–70 (Leiden, E. J. Brill, 1972), pp. 53–81.

"The Mission of the Church and the Future of Missions." In: George Johnston and Wolfgang Roth, eds., *The Church in the Modern World: Essays in Honour of James Sutherland Thomson* (Toronto, The Ryerson Press, 1967), pp. 154–170.

" 'Traditional Religions and Modern Culture.' " In: *Proceedings of the XIth International Congress of the International Association for the History of Religions*, vol. 1, The Impact of Modern Culture on Traditional Religions (Leiden, E. J. Brill, 1968), pp. 55–72.

"Secularity and the History of Religion." In: Albert Schlitzer, ed., *The Spirit and Power of Christian Secularity* (Notre Dame and London, University of Notre Dame Press, 1969), pp. 33–58. Discussion follows, pp. 59–70.

"University Studies of Religion in a Global Context." In: *Study of Religion in Indian Universities: A Report of the Consultation Held in Bangalore in September, 1967* ([Bangalore], Bangalore Press, n.d. [1970]), pp. 74–87.

"Participation: The Changing Christian Role in Other Cultures," *Occasional Bulletin*, Missionary Research Library, New York, 20:4 (1969) 1–13
   Reprinted: *Religion and Society*, Bangalore, 17:1 (1970) 56–74; and in abridged form in Gerald H. Anderson and Thomas F. Stransky, eds., *Mission Trends No. 2* (New York, Paulist Press, and Grand Rapids, Eerdmans, 1975), pp. 218–229.

"The Study of Religion and the Study of the Bible," *Journal of the American Academy of Religion* 39 (1971) 131–140.

"A Human View of Truth," *SR: Studies in Religion/Sciences Religieuses* 1 (1971) 6–24.
   Reprinted: John Hick, ed., *Truth and Dialogue: The Relationship between World Religions* (London, Sheldon Press, 1974); *Truth and Dialogue in World Religions: Conflicting Truth-Claims* (Philadelphia, Westminster Press, 1974), pp. 20–44, with a new addendum, "Conflicting Truth-Claims: A Rejoinder," *ibid.*, pp. 156–162.

"Programme Notes for a Mitigated Cacophony" (a review article on R. C. Zaehner, *Concordant Discord*, 1970), *The Journal of Religion* 53 (1973) 377–381.

"On 'Dialogue and Faith': A Rejoinder" [to Eric J. Sharpe, "Dialogue and Faith," in the same issue], *Religion* 3 (1973) 106–114.

" 'The Finger That Points to the Moon': Reply to Per Kværne"

[Kværne, " 'Comparative Religion: Whither—and Why?' A Reply to Wilfred Cantwell Smith," in the same issue], *Temenos*, Helsinki, 9 (1973) 169–172.

"World Religions" (in the section, "What's in Store for '74? Looking Ahead in Various Areas of Contemporary Life"), *The Christian Century*, 91:1 (1974) 16.

"Religion as Symbolism," introduction to Propaedia, part 8, "Religion," *Encyclopaedia Britannica*, 15th ed. (Chicago, Encyclopaedia Britannica, 1974), vol. 1, pp. 498–500.

"Methodology and the Study of Religion: Some Misgivings," in: Robert D. Baird, ed., *Methodological Issues in Religious Studies* (Chico, Calif., New Horizons Press, 1975), pp. 1–25 ("Discussion", pp. 25–30). "Is the Comparative Study of Religion Possible? Panel Discussion," with Jacob Neusner, Hans H. Penner, ibid., pp. 95–109. "Rejoinder," pp. 123–124.

ARTICLES ON EDUCATION, AREA STUDIES, AND
SOCIAL CONCERN GENERALLY

"Achievement Tests in History," *Education*, Lucknow, 24:1 (1945) 57–62.

"Objective Test in History," *Education*, Lucknow, 24:2 (1945) 53–60.
Reprinted: *The Punjab Educational Journal*, Lahore, 29 (1944) 309–313, 336–345.

"The Place of Oriental Studies in a Western University," *Diogenes* no. 16 (1956) 104–111.
Translated into: French (1956), German (1957), and Spanish (1958).

"The Christian and the Near East Crisis," *The British Weekly*, London, 138, no. 3658 (December 20, 1956) 5.
Also published in: *The Presbyterian Record*, Toronto, 82:1 (January, 1957) 16–17.

"The YMCA and the Present," *Bulletin*, National Council of Young Men's Christian Associations of Canada, Toronto, 34:4 (June, 1960) 3–5.

"Non-Western Studies: The Religious Approach." In: *A Report on an Invitational Conference on the Study of Religion in the State University, Held October 23–25, 1964 at Indiana University Medical Center* (New Haven, The Society for Religion in Higher Education, [1965]), pp. 50–62. Comments and discussion follow, pp. 62–67.

"The Islamic Near East: Intellectual Role of Librarianship," *Library Quarterly* 35 (1965) 283–294. Discussion follows, pp. 294–297.
Reprinted: Tsuen-Hsuin Tsien and Howard W. Winger, eds., *Area Studies and the Library* (Chicago & London, The University of Chicago Press, 1966), pp. 81–92 (92–95).

Orientalism and Truth: A Public Lecture in Honor of T. Cuyler Young, Horatio Whitridge Garrett Professor of Persian Language and History, Chairman of the Department of Oriental Studies (pamphlet). Princeton, Program in Near Eastern Studies, Princeton University, 1969. 16 pp.

"Objectivity and the Humane Sciences: A New Proposal," *Transactions of the Royal Society of Canada* (Ottawa, Royal Society of Canada, 1975), 4/12 (1974) 81–102.

Articles on Islamic Subjects

"The Mughal Empire and the Middle Class: A Hypothesis," *Islamic Culture*, Hyderabad, 18 (1944) 349–363.

"Lower-Class Uprisings in the Mughal Empire," *Islamic Culture*, Hyderabad, 20 (1946) 21–40.

"The Muslim World." In: *One Family* (Toronto, Missionary Society of the Church of England in Canada, 2 vols, 1947–48), vol. 2, pp. 27–32.

"Hyderabad: Muslim Tragedy," *Middle East Journal* 4 (1950) 27–51.

"The Muslims and the West," *Foreign Policy Bulletin*, New York, 31:2 (October, 1951), 5–7.

"Islam Confronted by Western Secularism, (A): Revolutionary Reaction." In: Dorothea Steelye Franck, ed., *Islam in the Modern World: A Series of Addresses Presented at the Fifth Annual Conference on Middle East Affairs, Sponsored by the Middle East Institute* (Washington, Middle East Institute, 1951), pp. 19–30.
Translated into: Arabic (1953).

"Modern Turkey—Islamic Reformation?" *Islamic Culture*, Hyderabad, 25:1 (1952) 155–186.
Reprinted in abridged form, with comments: *Die Welt des Islams*, n.F. 3 (1954) 269–273.
Translated into: Turkish (1953).

"Pakistan," *Collier's Encyclopedia*, 1953.

"The Institute of Islamic Studies [McGill University]," *The Islamic Literature*, Lahore, 5 (1953) 173–176.

"The Importance of Muhammad" (review article), *The Canadian Forum*, September, 1954, 135–136.

"The Intellectuals in the Modern Development of the Islamic World." In: Sydney Nettleton Fisher, ed., *Social Forces in the Middle East* (Ithaca, Cornell University Press, 1955), pp. 190–204.

"Propaganda (Muslim)," *Twentieth Century Encyclopaedia of Religious Knowledge* (Grand Rapids, Baker, 2 vols., 1955), II, 767–768.

"Ahmadiyyah," *Encyclopaedia of Islam*, new edition (Leiden and London, E. J. Brill, 1956).
Translated into: French (1956).

"Amir Ali, Sayyid," *Encyclopaedia of Islam*, new edition (Leiden and London, E. J. Brill, 1956).
Translated into: French (1956).

The Muslim World (pamphlet, Current Affairs for the Canadian Forces series, vol. 10, no. 4). Ottawa, Bureau of Current Affairs, Department of National Defense, 1956. 26 pp.
Translated into: French (1956).

"Islam in the Modern World," *Current History* 32 (1957) 321–325.
Reprinted: *Enterprise*, Karachi, January 4, 1958; *Morning News*, Karachi, April 12, 1959.

"Independence Day in Indonesia," *The McGill News*, Montreal, Winter, 1957, pp. 23–24.

"Aga Khan III," *Encyclopedia Americana*, 1958.

"Law and Ijtihad in Islam: Some Considerations on Their Relation to Each Other and to Ultimate and Immediate Problems," *Dawn*, Karachi, January 5, 1958.
Reprinted: *Pakistan Quarterly*, Karachi, 8 (1958) 29–31, 63; also in *International Islamic Colloquium Papers: December 29, 1957–January 8, 1958* (Lahore, Panjab University Press, 1960), pp. 111–114.
Translated into: Urdu (1958), Arabic (1960).

"India, Religion and Philosophy: Islam," *Encyclopedia Americana*, 1960.
Reprinted: W. Norman Brown, ed., *India, Pakistan, Ceylon*, revised edition (Philadelphia, University of Pennsylvania Press; London, Oxford University Press, [1964]), pp. 104–107.

"Modern Muslim Historical Writing in English." In: C. H. Phillips, ed., *Historians of India, Pakistan and Ceylon* (Historical Writing on the Peoples of Asia, 1) (London, Oxford University Press, 1961), pp. 319–331.

"The Comparative Study of Religion in General and the Study of Islam as a Religion in Particular." In: *Colloque sur la sociologie musulmane: Actes, 11–14 septembre 1961* (Correspondance d'Orient, 5) (Bruxelles, Publications du Centre pour l'étude des problèmes du monde musulman contemporain, [1962]), pp. 217–231.

"Iblis," *Encyclopaedia Britannica*, 1962.

"The Historical Development in Islam of the Concept of Islam as an Historical Development." In: Bernard Lewis and P. M. Holt, eds., *Historians of the Middle East* (Historical Writing on the Peoples of Asia, 4) (London, Oxford University Press, 1962), pp. 484–502.

"The 'Ulamā' in Indian Politics." In: C. H. Phillips, ed., *Politics and Society in India* (London, George Allen & Unwin Ltd., 1963), pp. 39–51.

"Druze," *Encyclopaedia Britannica*, 1963.

"Koran (Qur'an)," *Encyclopaedia Britannica*, 1964.

"The Concept of Shari'a among Some Mutakallimun." In: George Makdisi, ed., *Arabic and Islamic Studies in Honor of Hamilton A. R. Gibb* (Leiden, E. J. Brill, 1965), pp. 581–602.

"The Crystallization of Religious Communities in Mughul India." In: Mōjtaba Minovi and Iraj Afshar, eds., *Yād-Nāme-ye-Īrāni-ye Minorsky* (Ganjīne-ye Taḥqīqāt-e Īrāni, no. 57; Publications of Tehran University, no. 1241) (Tehran, Intishārāt Dāneshgāh, 1969), pp. 197–220.

"The End is Near" [annotated translation from Urdu of Siddīq Ḥasan Khān, reputed author, *Iqtirāb al-Sā'ah*]. Published anonymously in: Aziz Ahmad and G. E. von Grunebaum, eds., *Muslim Self-Statement in India and Pakistan 1857–1968* (Wiesbaden, Otto Harrassowitz, 1970), pp. 85–89.

PUBLICATIONS IN TRANSLATION

ARABIC

("Islam Confronted by Western Secularism: Revolutionary Reaction," 1951) "Al-Islām yuwājih al-'ilmānīyah al-gharbīyah," trans. Isḥāq Mūsá al-Ḥusaynī with notes by 'Alī 'Abd al-Wāḥid Wāfī. In: Philip K. Hitti et al., *Al-Islām fī naẓar al-Gharb* (Bayrūt, Dār Bayrūt, 1953), pp. 38–59.

(*Islam in Modern History*, 1957, partial translation) "Al-Islām wa al-taṭawwur," "Al-Islām fī al-ta'rīkh al-ḥadīth." In: Niqūlā Ziyādah, ed.,

Dirāsāt Islāmīyah (Bayrūt, Dār al-Andalus, 1960), pp. 295–402.

(*Islam in Modern History,* 1957, pirated edition, abridged) *Al-Islām fī al-taʾrīkh al-ḥadīth* (Kutub siyāsīyah, 163). Cairo, n.d. [1960].

(*Islam in Modern History,* 1957, authorized translation) *Al-Islām fī al-taʾrīkh al-ḥadīth,* trans. and with a foreword by Dr. M. Kāmil Ḥusayn. Bayrūt, al-Muʾassasah al-ʿArabīyah li-al-baḥth wa-al-nashr, 1975.

FRENCH

("The Place of Oriental Studies in a Western University," 1956) "Le Rôle de l'université dans un monde à civilisations multiples," *Diogène,* Paris, 16 (1956) 3–13. Traduit par Nicole Laming.

("Ahmadiyyah," 1956) "Ahmadiyyah," *Encyclopédie de l'Islam,* nouvelle édition, Leiden and Paris, E. J. Brill, 1956.

("Amir Ali, Sayyid," 1956) "Amir Ali, Sayyid," *Encyclopédie de l'Islam,* nouvelle édition, Leiden and Paris, E. J. Brill, 1956.

(*The Muslim World,* 1956) *Le monde musulman,* (brochure, in the series Actualités, revue destinée aux forces canadiennes, vol. 10, no. 4). Ottawa, Bureau des actualités, Ministère de la Défense nationale, 1956. 26 pp.

(*Islam in Modern History,* 1957) *L'Islam dans le monde moderne,* préface et traduction de A. Guimbretière. Paris, Payot, 1962.

GERMAN

("The Place of Oriental Studies in a Western University," 1956) "Die Orientwissenschaft an einer Universität des Westens," *Diogenes,* Köln-Marienburg, 16 (1957) 522–530.

(*Islam in Modern History,* 1957) *Der Islam in der Gegenwart,* übertragen von Hermann Stiehl. Frankfurt und Hamburg, Fischer Bücherei, 1963.

("Comparative Religion: Whither—and Why?" 1959) "Vergleichende Religionswissenschaft: wohin—warum?" übersetzt von Dr. Elisabeth Schmitz-Mayr-Harting. In: Mircea Eliade und Joseph M. Kitagawa, hrsg., *Grundfragen der Religionswissenschaft: Acht Studien* (Salzburg, Otto Müller Verlag, 1963), pp. 75–105, 239–256.

("Mankind's Religiously Divided History Approaches Self-Conscious-

ness," 1964) "Das erwachende Selbstbewusstsein von der geschicht-
lichen Vielfalt der Religionen," von Hans-Joachim Klimkeit ins
Deutsche übertragen. In: Rudolf Thomas, hrsg., *Religion und
Religionen: Festschrift für Gustav Mensching zu seinem 65.
Geburtstag* (Bonn, Ludwig Rohrscheid Verlag, 1967), pp. 190–208.

INDONESIAN

(*Islam in Modern History*, 1957) *Islam dalam sedjarah modern*, diter-
djemahkan oleh Abusalamah. Djakarta, Bhratara, 2 vols., 1962–64.

JAPANESE

("Comparative Religion: Whither—and Why?" 1959) "Korekara no
hikakushūkyōgaku no arikata." In: M. Eriāde, J. M. Kitagawa, hen.,
Shūkyōgaku nyumon, Kishimoto Hideo, kanyaku (Tokyo,
Tōkyō daigaku-shuppankai, 1962), pp. 47–84. Reprinted 1966.
"Shoshūykō no kyōryoku wa kanōka—Jinrui kyōdōtai e rekishi-teki
shimei-kan o" ["Is inter-religious co-operation possible? The prob-
lem of world community in historical perspective"], *Yomiuri
Shimbun*, Tokyo, January 9, 1966, p. 11. (Published only in
Japanese.)
(*Questions of Religious Truth*, 1967) *Shūkyo no shinri*, Kasai Minoru,
yaku. Tokyo, Riso Sha, 1971. (Shūkyo shisōsen sho, 10).
(*Islam in Modern History*, 1957) *Gendai ni okeru isuramu*, Nakamura
Kojiro, yaku. Tokyo, Kinokuniya, 1974.

SPANISH

("The Place of Oriental Studies in a Western University," 1956) "La
Función de la universidad en el complejo cultural de nuestro
mundo," *Diógenes*, Buenos Aires, 3 (1958) 3–12.

SWEDISH

(*Islam in Modern History*, 1957) *Islam i modern tid*, förord av H. S.
Nyberg, till svenska av Ulla Carlsted. Stockholm, Natur och Kultur,
1961.

(*The Faith of Other Men*, 1963) *Människor av annan tro*, till svenska av Axel Ljungberg och Alf Ahlberg. Stockholm, Natur och Kultur, 1965.

TURKISH

("Modern Turkey—Islamic Reformation?" 1952) "Modern Türkiye dini bir reforma mı gidiyor?" *İlâhiyat Fakültesi Dergisi*, Ankara, 2 (1953) 7–20.

URDU

"Ek Sawāl" ["A Question"], *Alīgaṛh Maygazīn*, Aligarh, 1955, pp. 81–83. (Published only in Urdu.)

(*Islam in Modern History*, 1957, partial translation) "Islām in mādarn hisṭarī: Ek bāb kā tarjamah," Mutarjim: Ẓiyā'u-l-Ḥasan Fārūqī, *Burhān*, Delhi, 14 (1958) 285–300, 349–364; 15 (1959) 45–58.

(*Islam in Modern History*, 1957, partial paraphrase) "Pākistān kī Islāmī riyāsat, parofaysar Ismith kī naẓar men," paraphrase by 'Abdu-r-Raḥmān 'Abd, *Chirāgh-i-Rāh* (Naẓariyah'-i Pākistān nambar), Karachi, 12:12 (December, 1960) 277–290. "Istidrāk," (Khrushīd Aḥmad), pp. 290–294. "Muẓākirah: Pākistān awr Islāmī naẓariyah—Dākṭar Wilfarayd Kaynṭwal Ismith" ["Discussion: Pakistan and Islamic theory"]. (Response to, and elaboration of, pp. 277–294; published only in Urdu.) pp. 363–366.

("Comparative Religion: Whither—and Why?" 1959) "Maẓhab kā taqābulī muṭāli'ah: Kiyūn awr kis ṭaraḥ," mutarjamah'-i jināb Sayyid Mubārizu-d-Dīn Ṣāḥib Raf'at awr Dākṭar Abū Naṣr Muḥammad Ṣāḥib Khālidī, *Burhān*, Delhi, 49 (1962) 197–216, 262–281, 348–355.

("Some Similarities and Differences between Christianity and Islam," 1959) "Islām awr Masīḥīyat—Kuchh farq, kuchh yaksāniyāṇ: Ek taqābulī muṭāli'ah'-i maẓāhib.' " In: *Dunyā-e Islām*, tarjamah'-i Sayyid Hāshimī Farīdābādī (Lahore, Maqbūl Akayḍamī, 1964), pp. 73–94.

Index

Africa: modernization in, 87; view of own past, 103
Ancient Near East, 56, 109
Andrews, C. F., 129
Anshei, J. C., 144
Aristotle, 9, 126
Aurobindo Ghose, 131
Averroes, 126

Barth, K., 111, 126
Behavioral sciences, 170–171
Bell, R., 31
bhakti, 124
Bible: as word of God, 24; study of as scripture, 44–56
Blachère, R., 31
Bonhoeffer, D., 76
Buber, M., 111, 131–132
Buddhism: as faith of Buddhists, 104, 171; as a developing tradition, 110, 122; among world religions, 109, 112; in *Britannica*, 103; and Tillich, 131
Bultmann, R., 54

China: religion and culture in, 64, 103; without mutually exclusive communities, 109, 136; "three teachings" in, 124
Christ as word of God, 24, 45
Christianity: as faith, 104, 122–123; as a developing tradition, 110;

early differentiation, 132; institutionalization, 70, truth of, 111; exclusivism, 10, 151; possibility of others' understanding, 147; among world religions, 108–129, 124; scripture in, 49–56; revelation in, 13; cross in, 104; study of, 44
Community: religious basis of, 12; as goal, 111; determines truth, 33–34; realized through dialogue, 153; vitiated by religious diversity, 10–11; vitiated by objectivity, 173–176; separate communities, 109
Comparative religion: three levels of, 102–108; interest in, 44; in Asian universities, 104; and mutual understanding, 146; as man's self-consciousness, 155; obligatory, 107; self-contradictory, 107–108
Conversion: change of community, 129–130; reorientation to own tradition, 132
Cragg, A. K., 36–37
Culture as a category, 61, 64–65

Darwin, C., 125
Dialogue: as a term, 127; participation, 132–135; in fashion, 150, 153; Christian-Jewish, 113 (trilogue, 124); Christian-Hindu, 151

Disciplines: as university fields, 75, 174–178; as seminary fields, 43
Divinity schools, role of, 100

Ecumenical movement, 5, 101, 113
Eliade, M., 168
Encyclopaedia Britannica, early treatment of Buddhism, 103
Encyclopaedia of Religon and Ethics, 139–140
Erman, A., 144
Exclusivism: and understanding, 104, 151; in Hinduism, 124–125

Faith: characterized, 67–72, 100, 142; and tradition, 70, 104; as object of description, 146–147; and reason, 100
Frankfort, H., 144
Freud, S., 125

Gandhi, M. K., 126, 129
al-Ghazzali, 126
Ghose, Aurobindo, 131
Gibb, H. A. R., 36
God: concept of, 43; knowledge of, 16–19; word of, 23–40
"Great" religions: period of emergence, 155; number half a dozen, 101
Greek thought, influence of, 8–9, 64, 126

Hadith, 45
Hammarskjöld, D., 70–71
von Hammer-Purgstall, J., 32
Handel, G. F., 38
Heber, R., 170–171
Heilsgeschichte, 112, 137
Heraclitus, 175
Herzl, T., 128
Hinduism: as faith of Hindus, 70, 73; names Indian culture, 64–66; as a developing tradition, 110; as a separate community, 109; and universalism, 124–125; and history, 67; temple in, 166–170
History: as process, 98–100; and origins, 110; as *Heilsgeschichte*, 137; and myth, 52–55; historian's task, 48, 97–98, 172; historical criticism, 52; Judaism unhistoricist, 68; Bible and the West, 55; Islamic and Christian historiography, 103–104; Hinduism unhistoricist, 67
History of religions: three levels in, 102–108; interest in, 44; in Asian universities, 104; and mutual understanding, 146; as man's self-consciousness, 155; obligatory, 107; distinguished from history of religion, 171
Humane: term defined, 160–161; implies breadth, 175–176; implies interpersonal, 177; implies freedom, 173; history of mankind, 135
Humanistic tradition: in West, 136; in Hinduism, 125
Humanities, 161, 177

India: man's quest in, 75; cow in, 69; separation of communities in, 109; stages in West's knowledge of, 166; modernity in, 78–95; and Pakistan, 124–125
Institutionalization, 70
Interrelations of religious communities: historical, 49, 107–109; contemporary, 124–134, 153–154
Islam: as faith of Muslims, 3, 67–68, 70, 118–122; as a separate community, 64–65, 109; as a developing tradition, 110, 118–120; among world religions, 108, 112, 136; trilogue in Spain, 124; and Hinduism, 124–125; and Christianity, 145; truth of, 111; outsider's understanding possible, 147; author's acquaintance with, 118–119; scripture in, 23–40, 45–46; mysticism in, 122
Isolationism, religious or cultural, 8, 11, 38, 107
Israel, State of, 86

Japan, plurality of membership in, 136
Jeffery, A., 31
Judaism: as faith of Jews, 68; as a separate community, 109; as a developing tradition, 110; among world religions, 112; and Christianity, 13, 113, 132; trilogue with Christianity and Islam, 124; scripture in, 49
Jung, C. G., 168

Kellerhals, E., 18
Kerr, C., 175
King, M. L., 126
Koran: see Qur'an
Kraemer, H., 131

Language controversy, India, 84, 89

Madurai, temple, 166–170
Maimonides, 126
Manichaeism, 109
Mankind: first emergence of, 163; distinctiveness of, 164–165; unity of, 39, 180; religious history of, 154–156; humane knowing, 177
Marcion, 48–49
Marx, K., 125; Marxists, 170
McGill University, 107, 141, 152
McLuhan, H. M., 52
Methodology: operation in a discipline, 175–177; more open in Asian studies, 44
Missionaries: defined as participants, 118–137; movement in crisis, 5–7, 150; Asian, in West, 127; in cooperation with others, 133–135
Modernity: as destructive of tradition, 61; as interiorized, 62; defined in Indian context, 78–95; related to wealth, 92; related to Westernization, 85–92
Muhammad: prophethood of, 28; inquirer's knowledge of, 32–33
Mutuality: of statement, 39, 145–148, 152–154; of world we are building, 113–114; of missions, 133–135; only method to know man, 177
Mysticism, in Islam, 122
Myth, 52–55

New Testament, 49, 99, 109
Newton, I., 9–10

Objectivity, 148, 160–180
Old Testament, 49, 99, 109
Orientalists: analytic mode, 47–48, 151; detachment, 165–171; information on Asia, 102–104; and area research, 141; and Bible, 56; and Qur'an, 24–25, 28, 31–38, 45; read by Asians, 145, 179

Pakistan: as ideological state, 66, 86, 120–121; as a test case, 69; and Hinduism, 124–125
Palestine: and Bible, 56; as source of Western religion, 64
Perry, E. F., 17–18
Personalism: as study of persons, 76, 113, 142; as stage of humane understanding, 166
Phenomenology, 76
"Primitive" religions, 144
Progress: idea of, 78–79; uncertainty of, 93–94

Qur'an: meaning of, 73; as word of God, 23–40; as scripture, 45–46

Radhakrishnan, S., 111, 131, 140, 151
Ramakrishna Mission, 127, 129, 134
Reformation, Protestant, 50–51
Religion: meaning faith, 146–147; without phenomena, 76; concept of, noun, 64–65, 68–69, 72, 109–110; major developing tradition, 101, 147; nature and origin of, 144
Religion, academic study of: three levels of, 102–108; as study of mankind, 154–155; as comparative, 140, 149, 151; as collaborative, 75–76, 127, 149; as detached, 148–149; in North American universities, 42–43; in Asian universities, 104
Ibn Rushd, 126

Sacred space, 167–170
Salvation, 17, 20–21
Science: first emergence of, 163; and objectivity, 161–162, 176; and verification, 163–164; and theology, 7–8, 18; potential of, 94, 98, 100
Scripture: concept of, 44–45; role in civilization, 47; in Christianity, 49–56; in Islam, 23–40, 45–46
Secularity: academic rationalism, 106, 149; Western, 71, 89; Indian, 86, 89
Seminaries: changing role of, 99–100; and university religion curricula, 43
Social sciences, 143, 170–171
Soviet Union as state, 86

Suzuki, D. T., 131
Symbols: function of, 74–75, 167–168;
    Exodus as, 49; Resurrection as, 49
Syncretism, 126

Temple, Madurai, 166–170
Theology: of religious diversity, 15–
    21; and interreligious co-opera-
    tion, 132–135; role of divinity
    school, 100
Tillich, P. J., 8, 111, 131
Tolstoy, L., 128
Toynbee, A. J., 128
Tradition: characterized, 68–72; rela-
    tion to faith, 104
Transcendence, 74
Truth: man's involvement with a
    thing, 171; life in accordance
    with scripture, 32; moral implica-
    tions of, 12; offered in dialogue,
    150; lies in future, 111; rational-
    ism as, 149; God concept as, 43;
    exclusive claims to, 13–14, 106;
    of Qur'an, 33–34; of temple, 167;
    vitiated by objectivity, 164–173;
    commitment of scholar to, 43

Understanding: defined, 172; in terms
    of intention, 168–169; as histo-
    rian's role, 97–98; and sharing,
    105–106, 146; possibility for out-
    sider, 147, 155, 173; as compara-
    tive, 107; idosyncratic under-
    standing, 175
United States as modern, 84–85
Universalism: goal of objectivity, 174;
    in Hinduism, 124–125
Universities: purpose of, 97–98, 100,
    102, 175; as detached, 148–149;
    Western tradition in, 152–153;
    career loyalties in, 175–176; in
    crisis, 160
Ussher, J., 53

Vietnam, Buddhists in, 69

Warren, M. A., 7
Wellhausen, J., 54
Westernization: scope of, 128; relation
    to modernization, 85–92; in flux,
    89–90